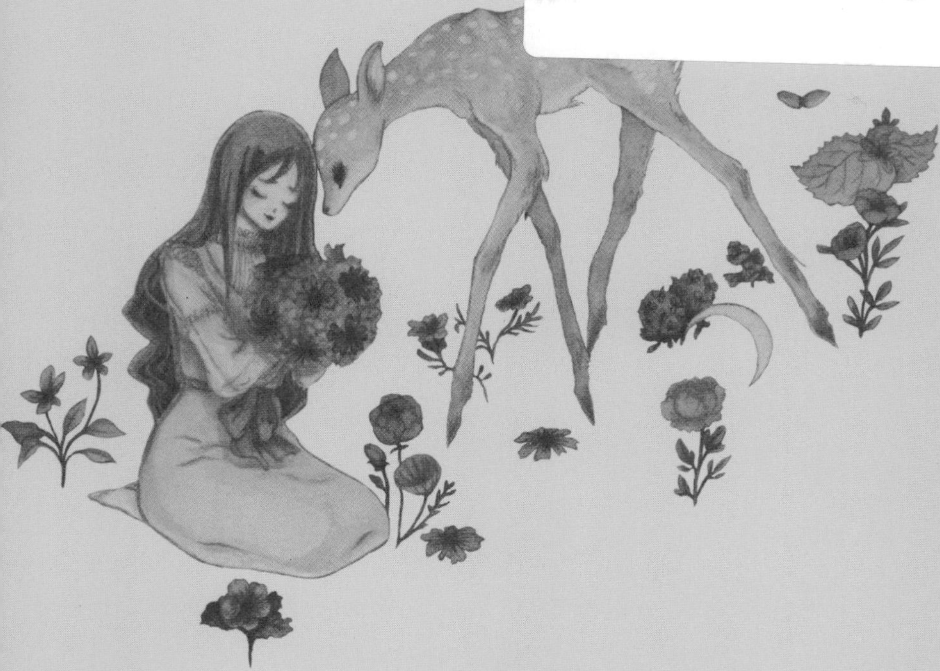

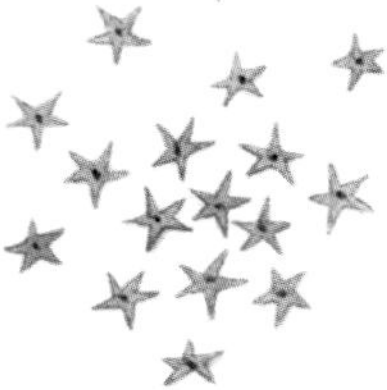

MINI MEDITATIONS ON

FRIENDSHIP

Enoki

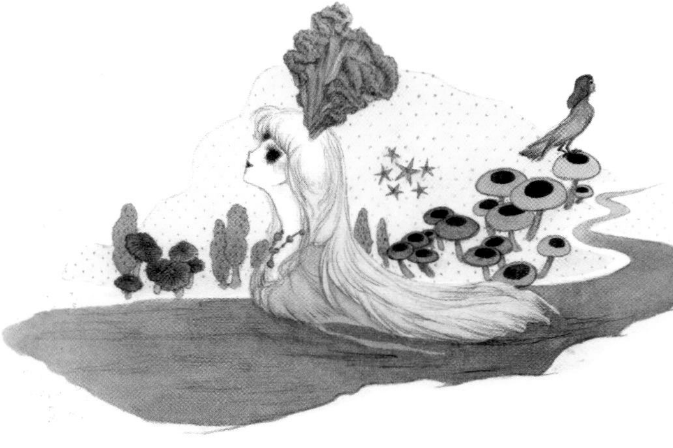

First published in 2019 by Liminal 11

Illustrated by Enoki

Book design by Mike Medaglia

Printed in Slovenia

ISBN 978-1-912634-09-5

10 9 8 7 6 5 4 3 2 1

www.liminal11.com

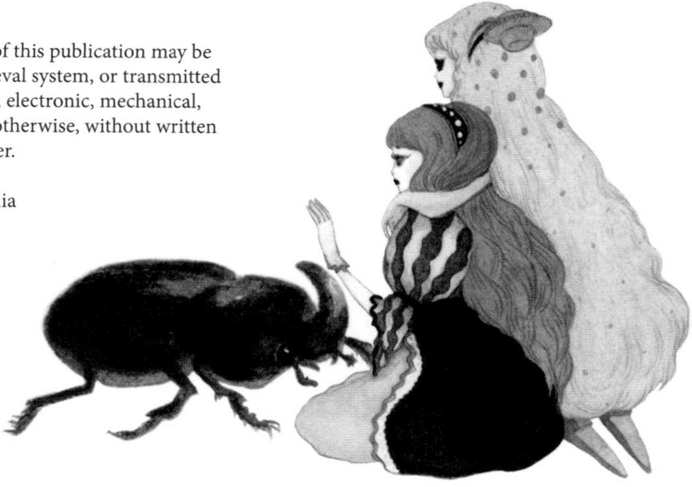

MINI MEDITATIONS ON

FRIENDSHIP

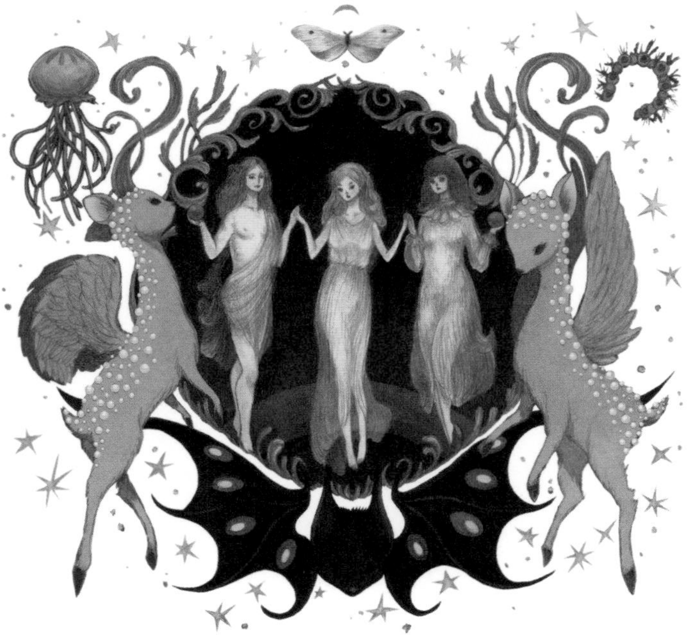

Enoki

INTRODUCTION

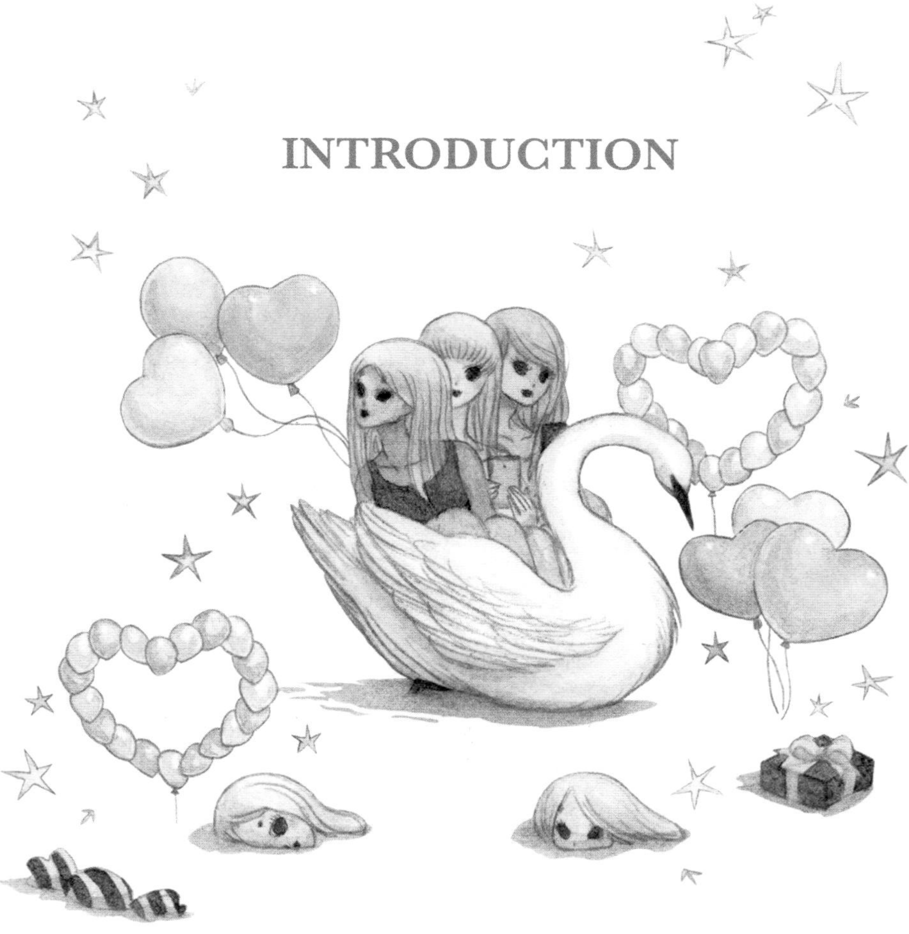

Dear Reader,

Thank you for picking up this book. In opening *Mini Meditations on Friendship*, you are about to meet my monsters! Or friends. My 'monster-friends', or the metaphor through which I have expressed contrasting extremes of my intimate experiences with friendships.

Friendships mean so many different things to people. As a child, I sought companionship over wandering alone in the playground, and some of the companions I met found a form of therapy through bullying me... though I no longer felt lonely, so it had been a mutually beneficial relationship. I hadn't known any better at the time, as I'm sure they didn't either. Fortunately, over time, my circumstances changed. I found myself in a new school where I was surprised to learn how mutual, exciting and fun friendship could be. Exploring life with friends has been fulfilling ever since. You enhance, support and learn through each other's journeys.

The contrast of these experiences taught me empathy and that what I had really been seeking in friendship was to be understood and to understand, opening my forays into Psychology and Philosophy. In our lifetime, we are all subject to a few revelations. One of mine was to recognise the monster who resides within myself; whose bite or bark when provoked are no longer necessary defence mechanisms. To accept that some of your own actions can cause difficulties for others, and to take responsibility for this. To swallow your pride and incant the magic of 'sorry' as a healer is so transformative.

Every individual has so much to learn, and for this reason it was important for me to selectively illustrate truths of diverse values from diverse walks of life. I hope you will discover in this book all the wisdom you need to strengthen the relationships you have. And if you are going through a difficult time with a friend – I want to say, 'hang in there!'. Life gets better when you actively seek to improve, and I hope this book will remind you of the power you have to transfigure yourself and the circumstances around you for the benefit of all.

And now, dear reader, it is time to meet my monsters...!

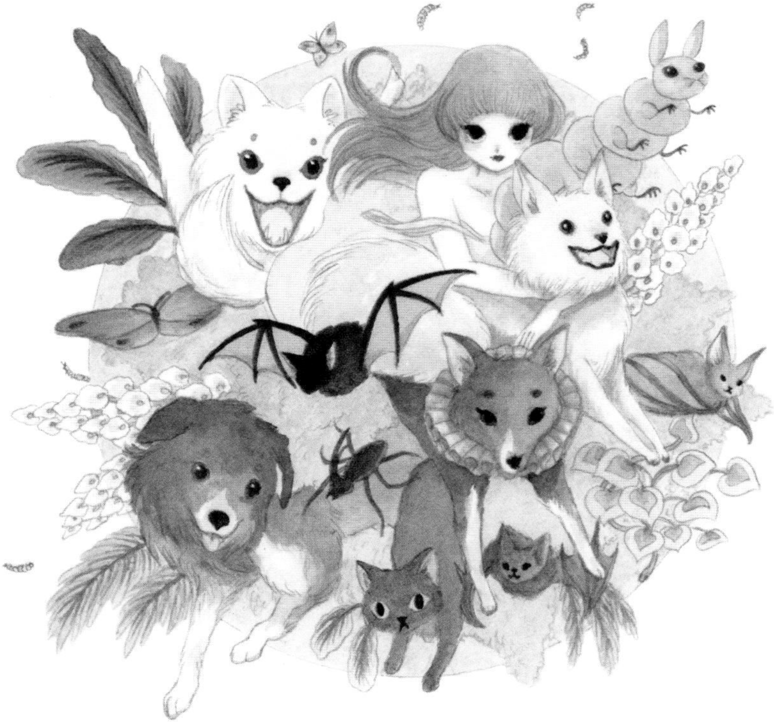

True friendship can
exist only between equals.

- PLATO

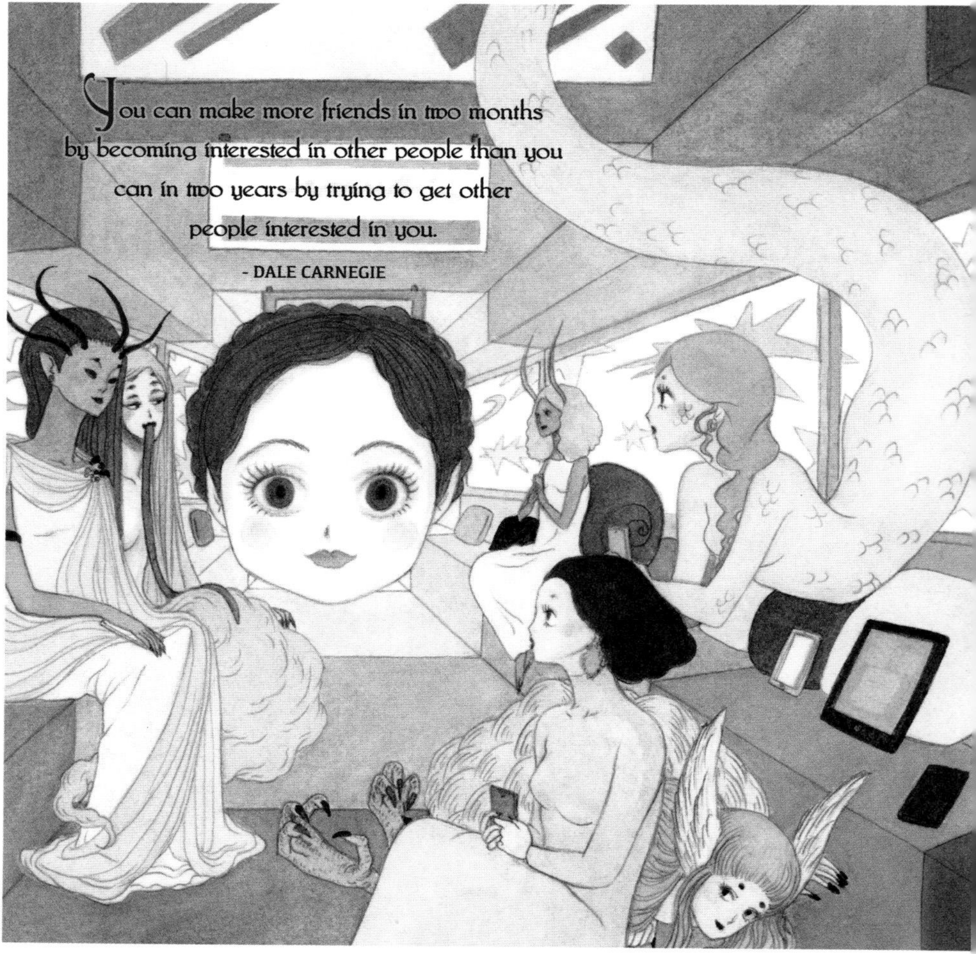
You can make more friends in two months by becoming interested in other people than you can in two years by trying to get other people interested in you.
- DALE CARNEGIE

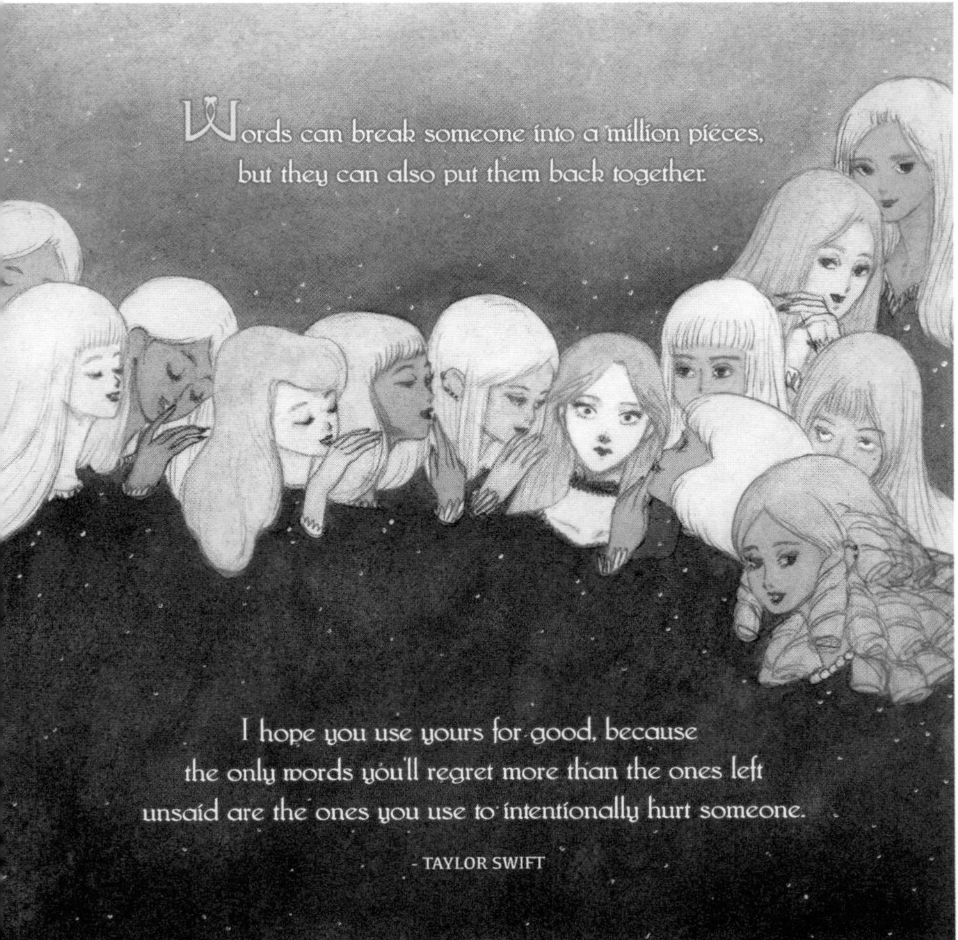

Words can break someone into a million pieces,
but they can also put them back together.

I hope you use yours for good, because
the only words you'll regret more than the ones left
unsaid are the ones you use to intentionally hurt someone.

\- TAYLOR SWIFT

Nobody sees a
flower- really; it is so small.
We haven't time and to see takes time,
like to have a friend takes time.

- GEORGIA O'KEEFFE

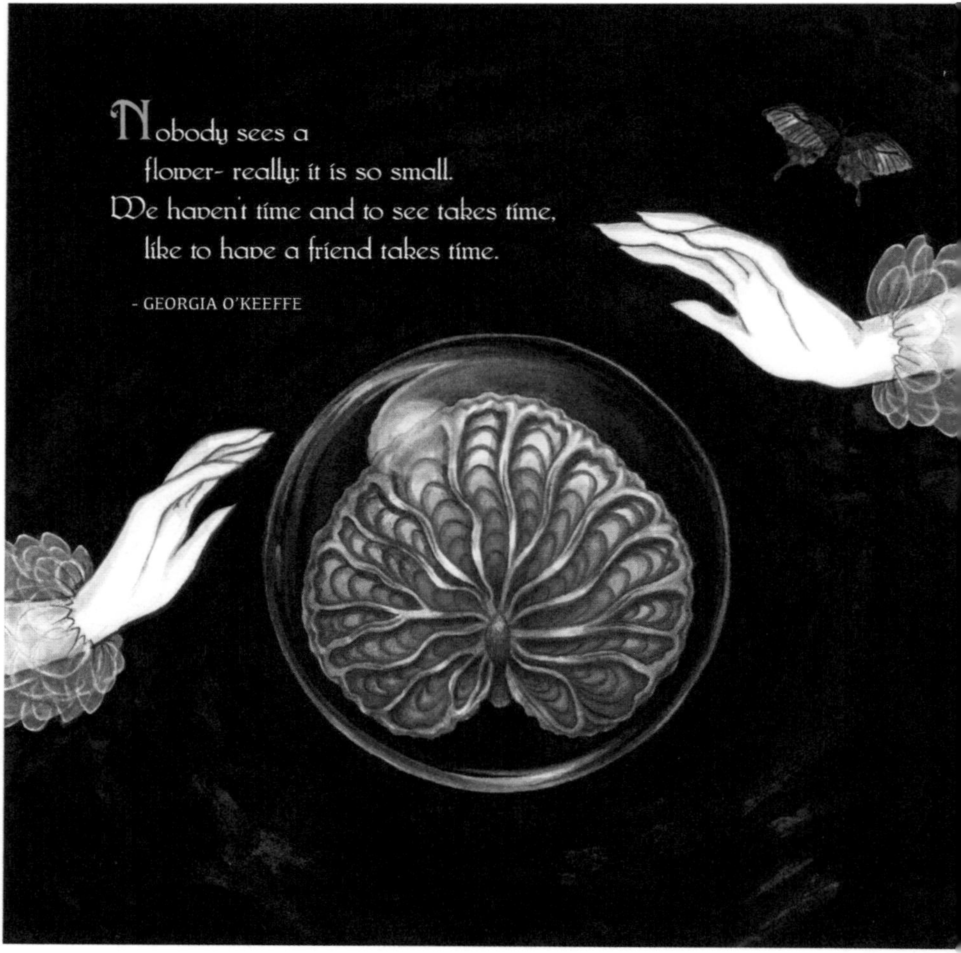

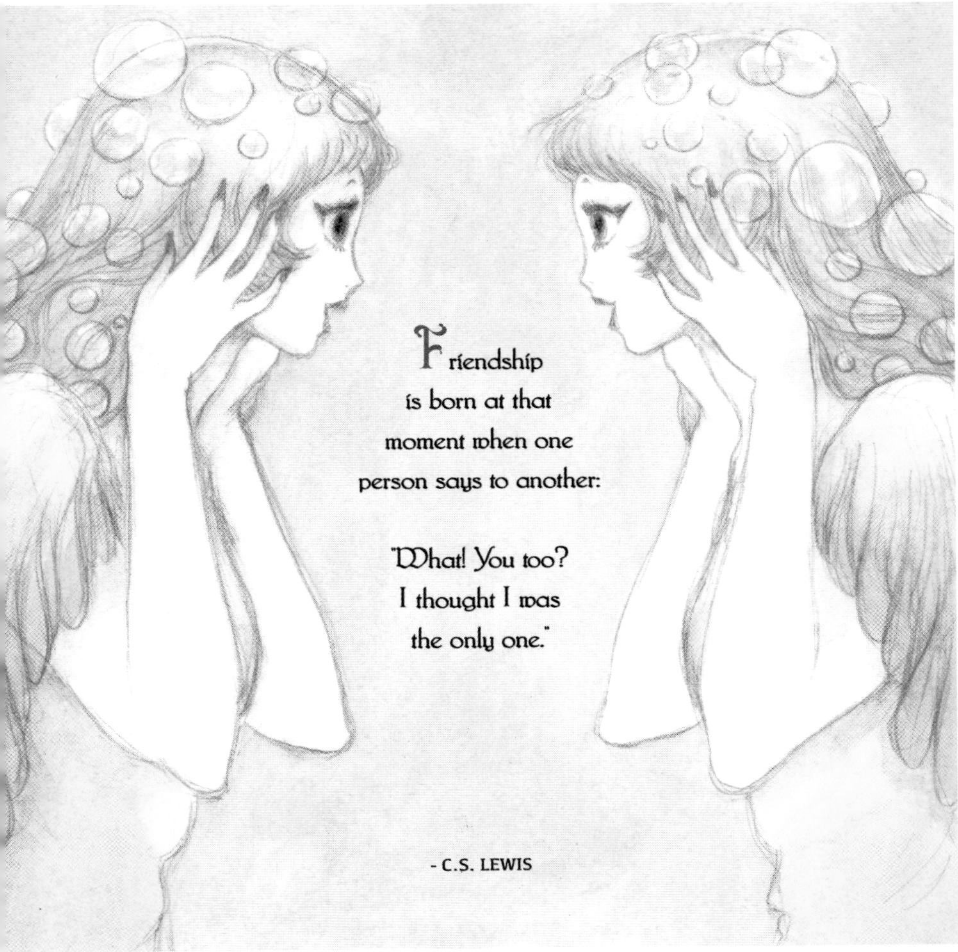

Friendship
is born at that
moment when one
person says to another:

"What! You too?
I thought I was
the only one."

- C.S. LEWIS

A single rose can be my garden...
A single friend, my world.

- LEO BUSCAGLIA

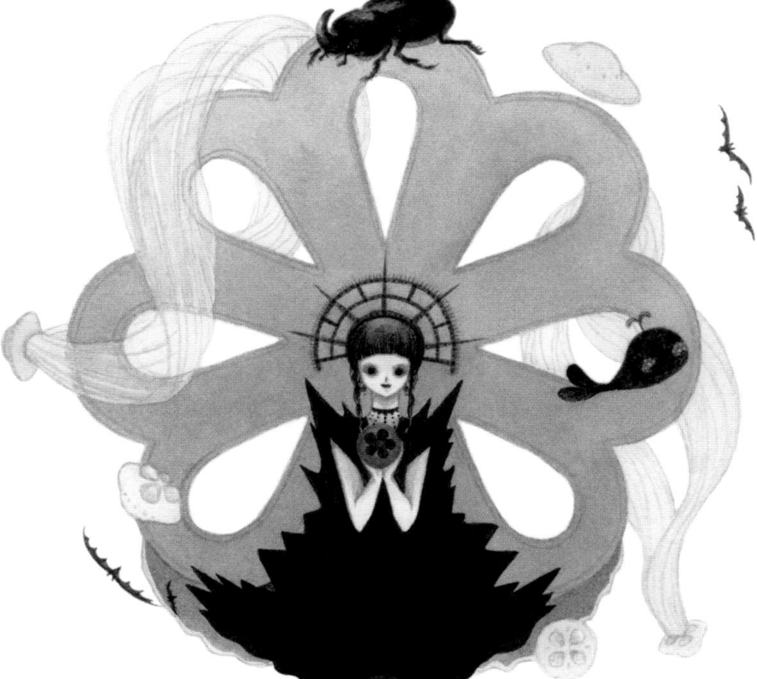

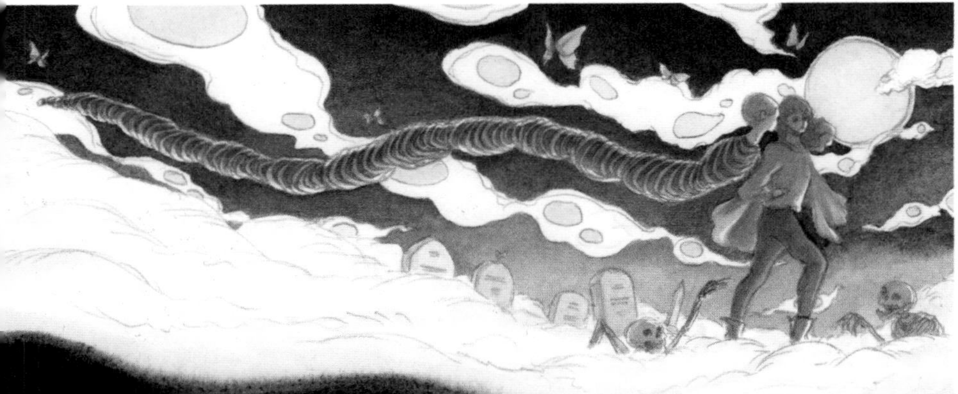

Every friendship travels at sometime
through the black valley of despair.
This tests every aspect of your affection.
You lose the attraction and the magic. Your sense of each
other darkens and your presence is sore.
If you can come through this time,
it can purify with your love,
and falsity and need will fall away.
It will bring you onto new
ground where affection
can grow again.

- JOHN O'DONOHUE

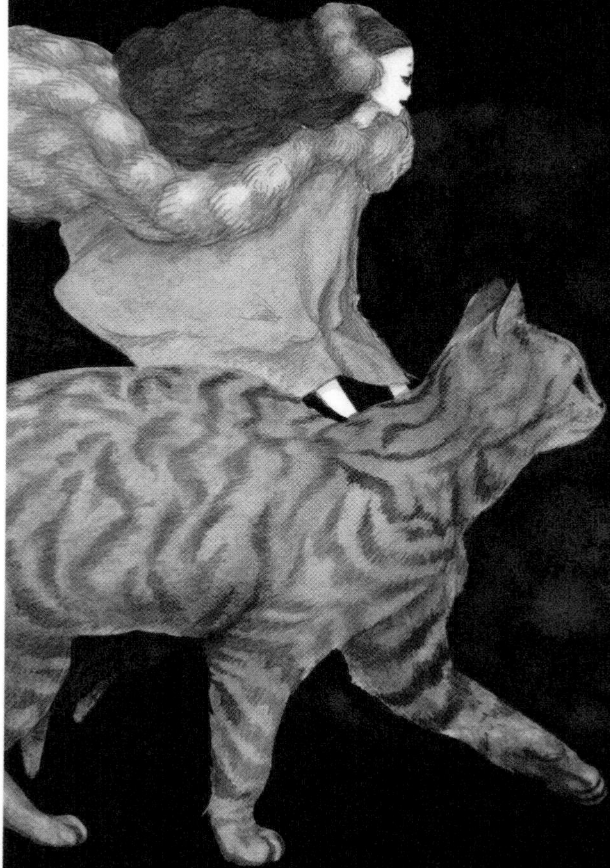

Don't walk behind me;
I may not lead.

Don't walk in front of me;
I may not follow.

Just walk beside me
and be my friend.

- ALBERT CAMUS

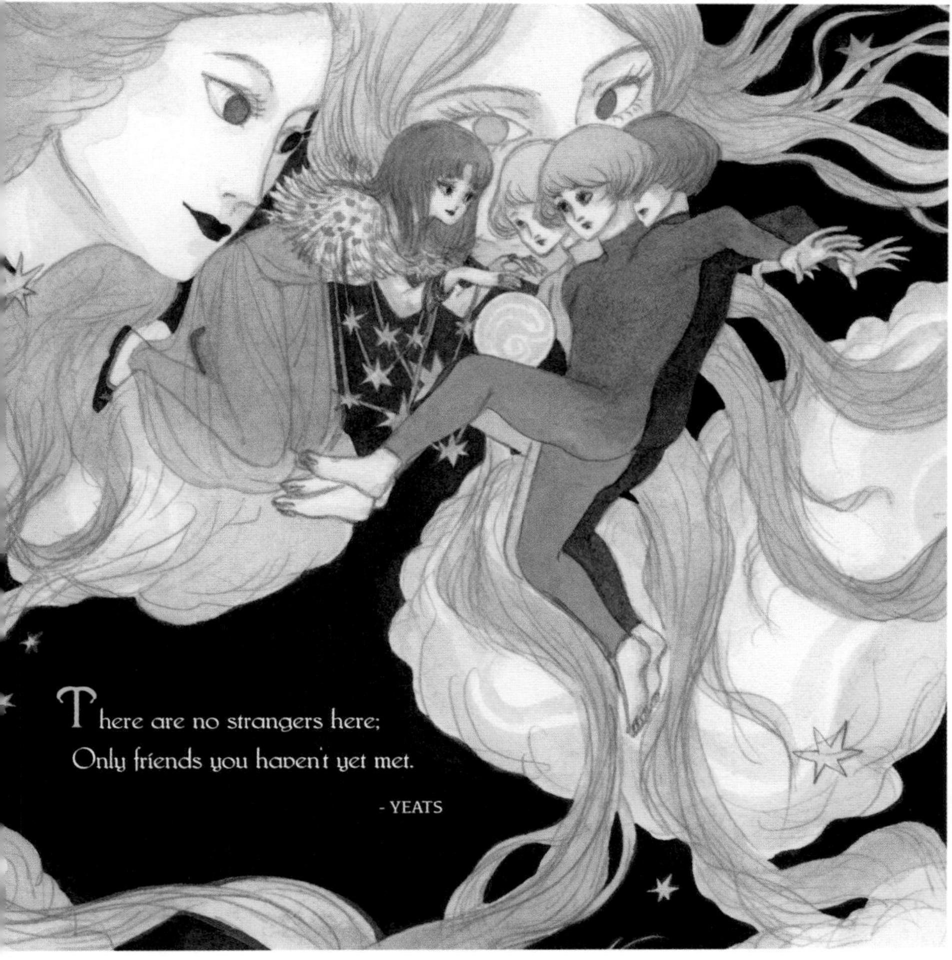

There are no strangers here;
Only friends you haven't yet met.

- YEATS

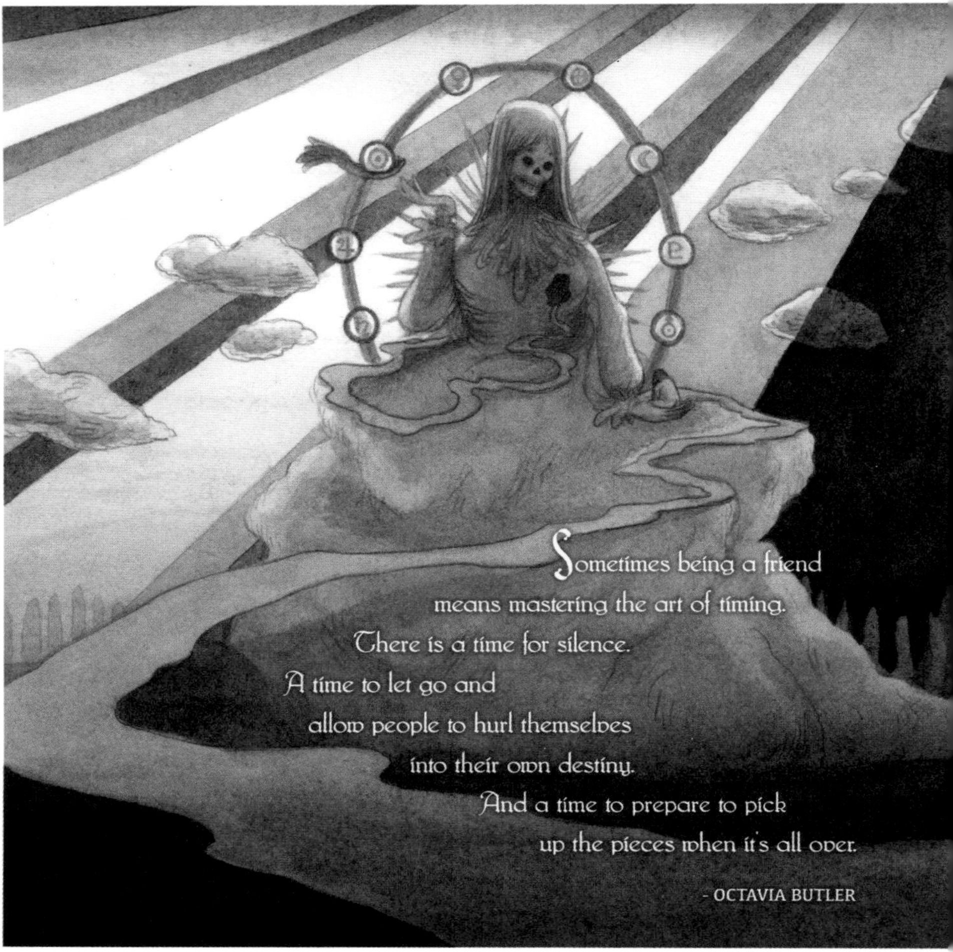

Sometimes being a friend
means mastering the art of timing.
There is a time for silence.
A time to let go and
allow people to hurl themselves
into their own destiny.
And a time to prepare to pick
up the pieces when it's all over.

- OCTAVIA BUTLER

What good
are friends if they
can't do you
any good?

- ANTON SZANDOR LAVEY

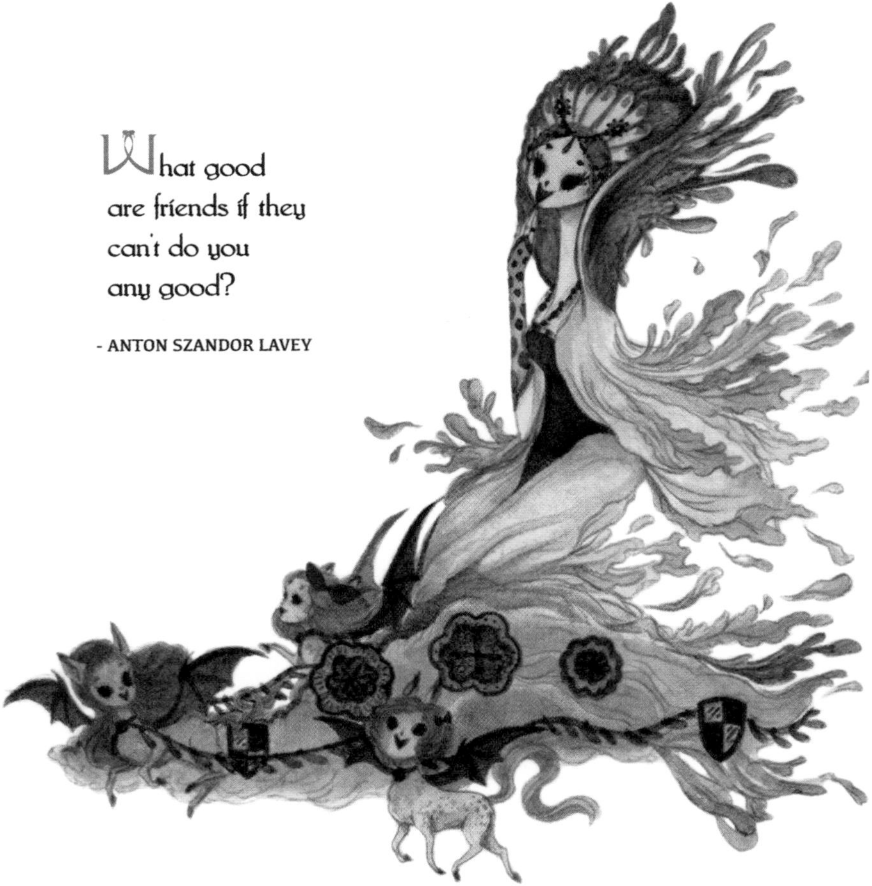

Be someone that nurtures,
and if there's someone in your class
that maybe doesn't have a lot of friends,

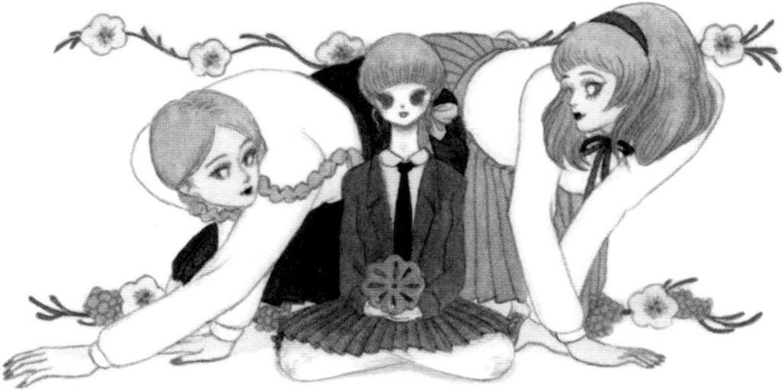

be the person that sits with them in the
cafeteria sometimes; be the bigger person.

- LADY GAGA

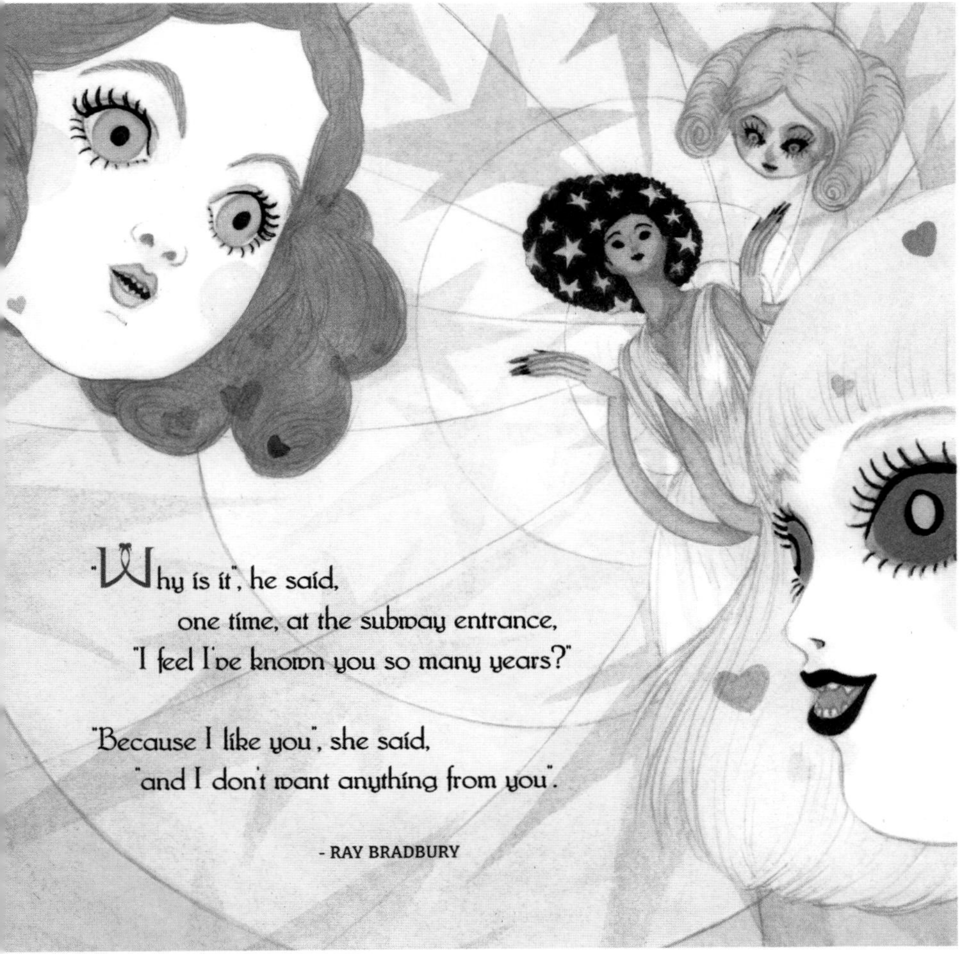

"Why is it", he said,
one time, at the subway entrance,
"I feel I've known you so many years?"

"Because I like you", she said,
"and I don't want anything from you".

- RAY BRADBURY

The only way to
have a friend
is to be one.

- RALPH WALDO EMERSON

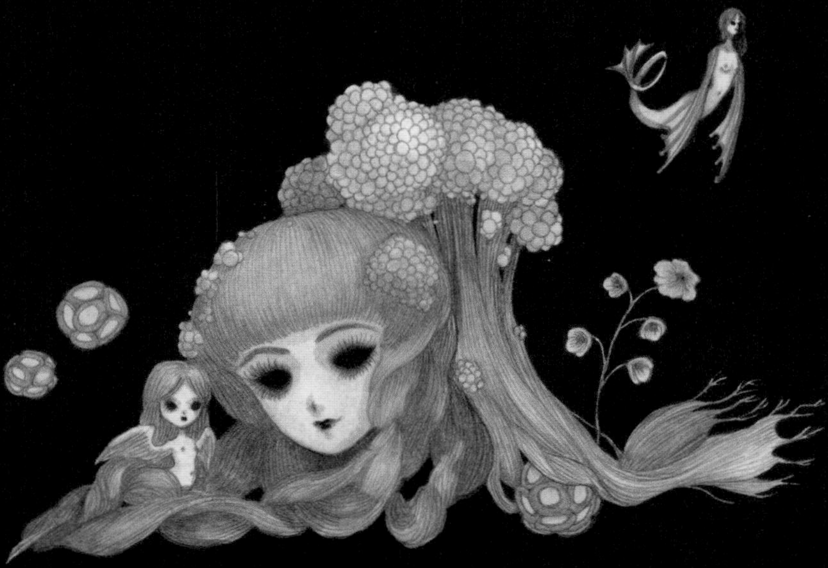

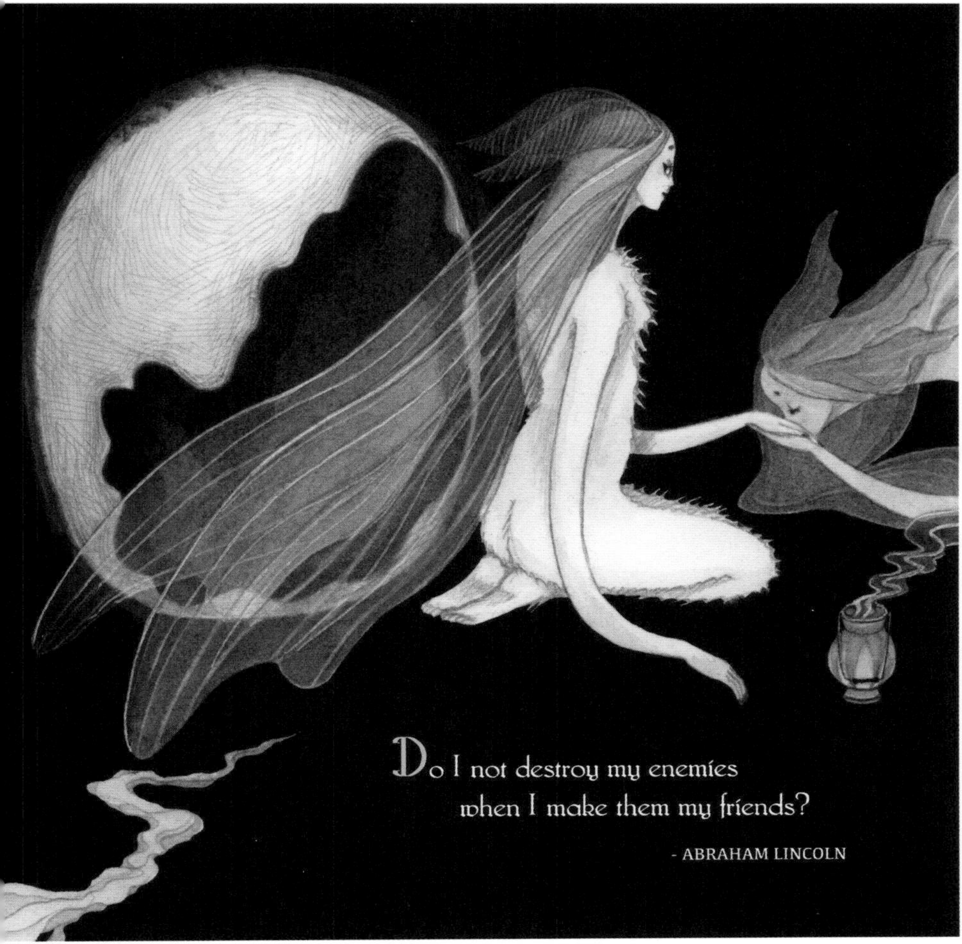
Do I not destroy my enemies
when I make them my friends?
- ABRAHAM LINCOLN

A true friend unbosoms freely, advises justly, assists readily, adventures boldy, takes all patiently, defends courageously, and continues a friend unchangeably.

- WILLIAM PENN

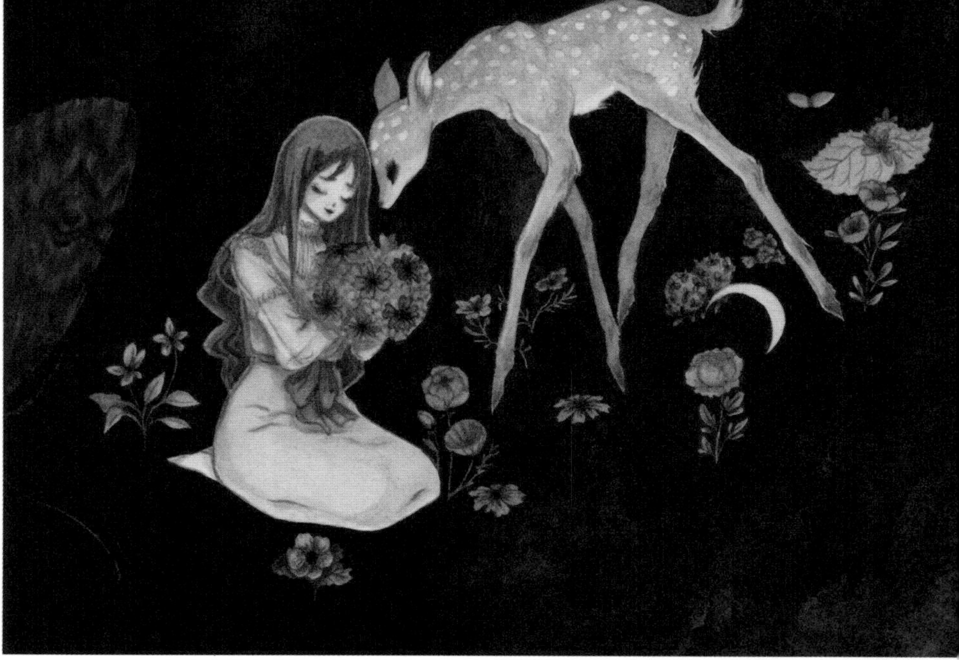

No person is your friend
who demands your silence,
or denies your right to grow.

- ALICE WALKER

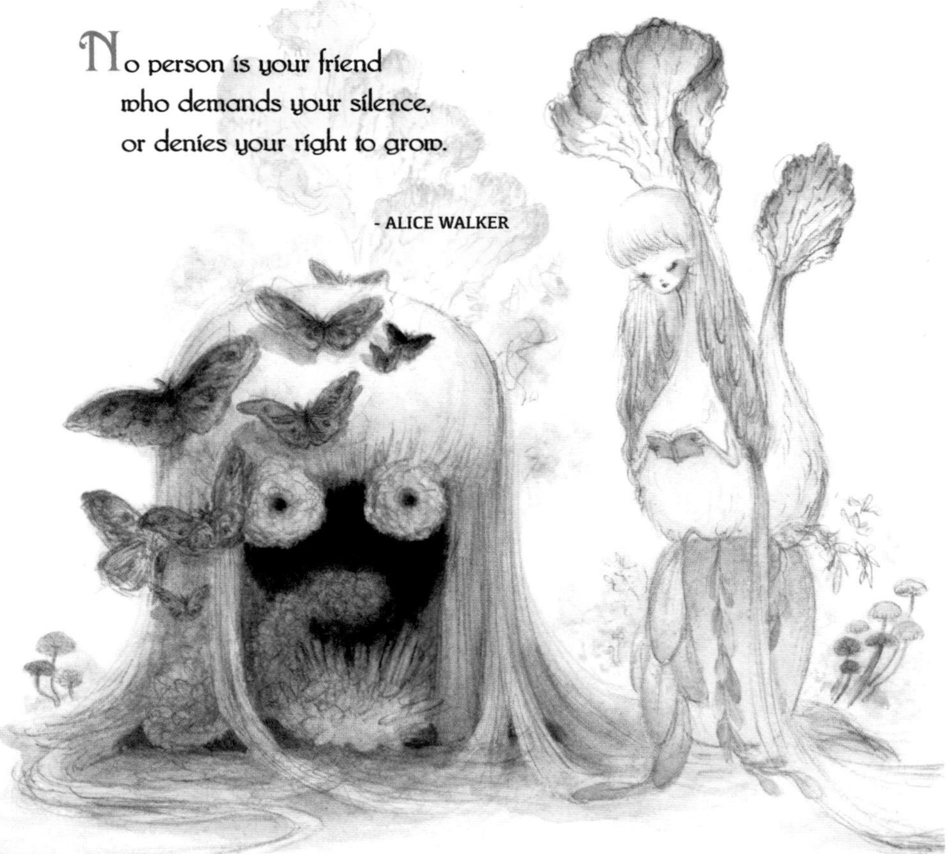

We checked ourselves in the mirror before we left.
We were flshed and a little rumpled, but in a good way.
We looked vibrant, wild, happy.

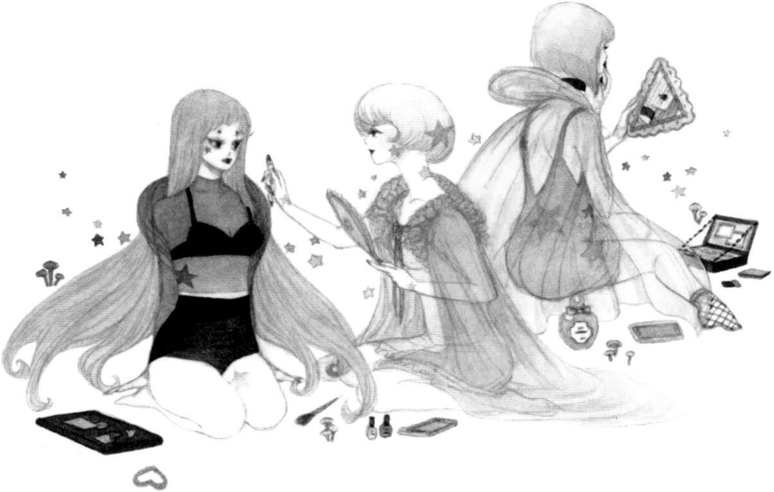

The hair and the clothes and the makeup made me feel like
someone new, but the happy is what made me unrecognisable.

- ALLIE LARKIN

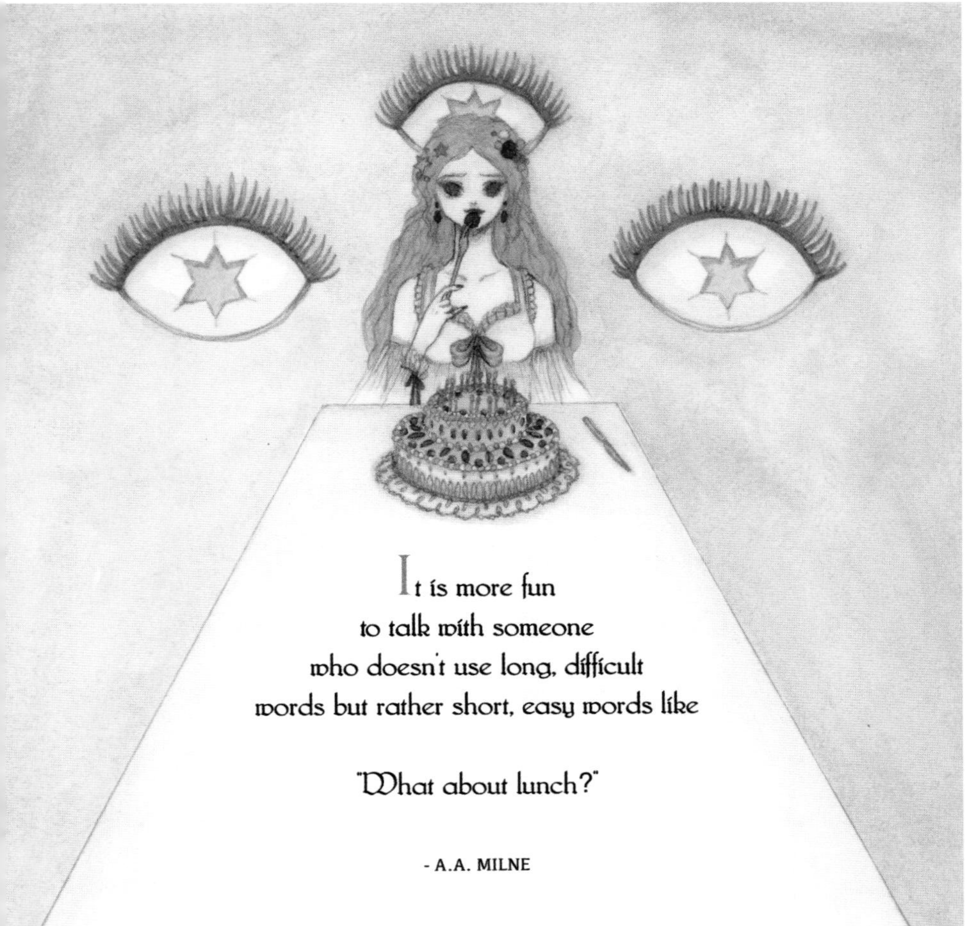

It is more fun
to talk with someone
who doesn't use long, difficult
words but rather short, easy words like

"What about lunch?"

- A.A. MILNE

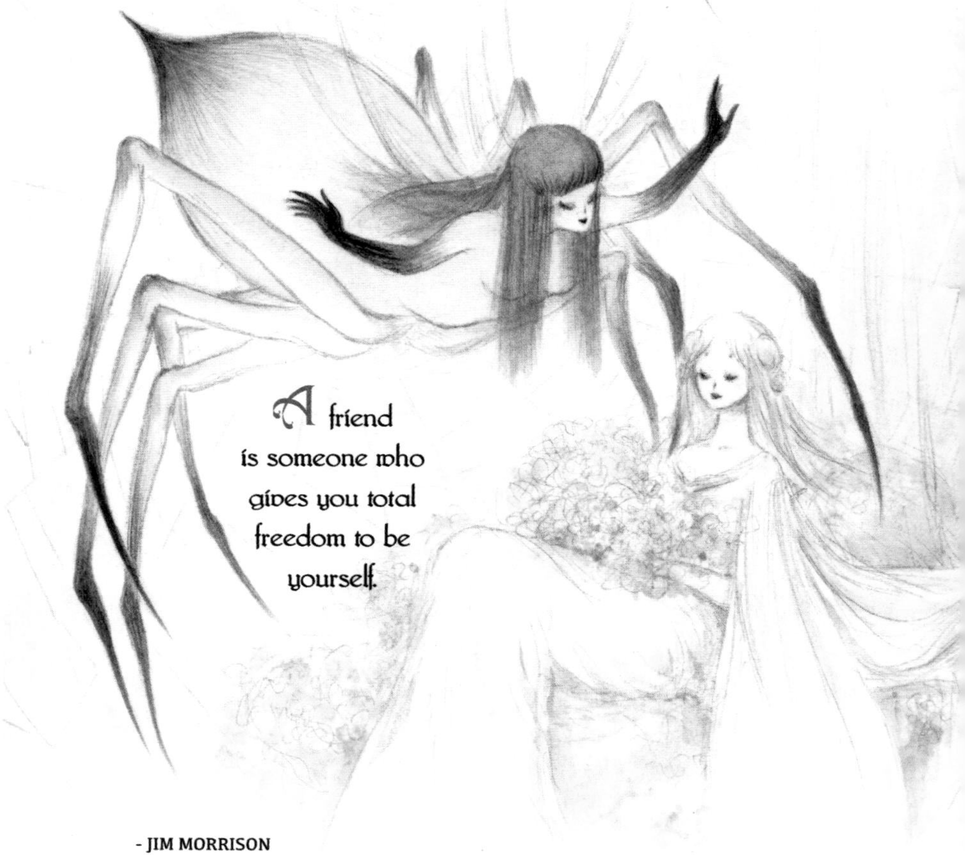

A friend
is someone who
gives you total
freedom to be
yourself.

- JIM MORRISON

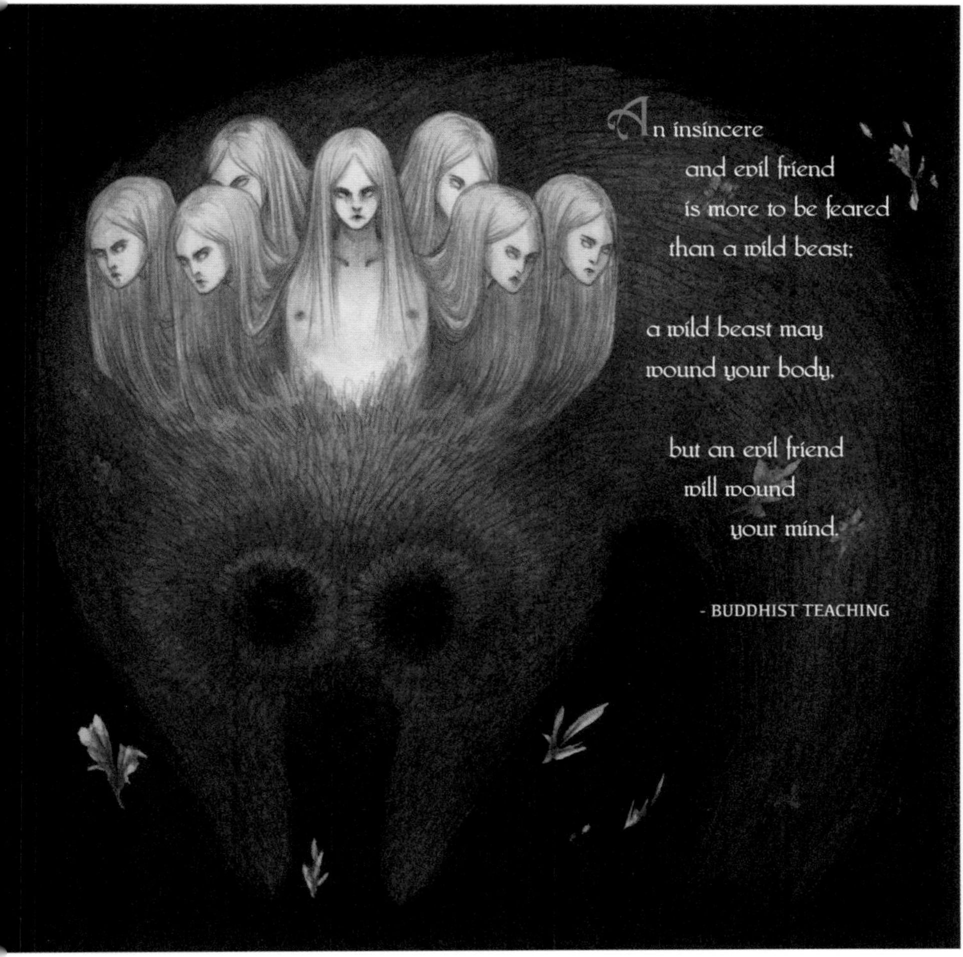

An insincere
and evil friend
is more to be feared
than a wild beast;

a wild beast may
wound your body,

but an evil friend
will wound
your mind.

- BUDDHIST TEACHING

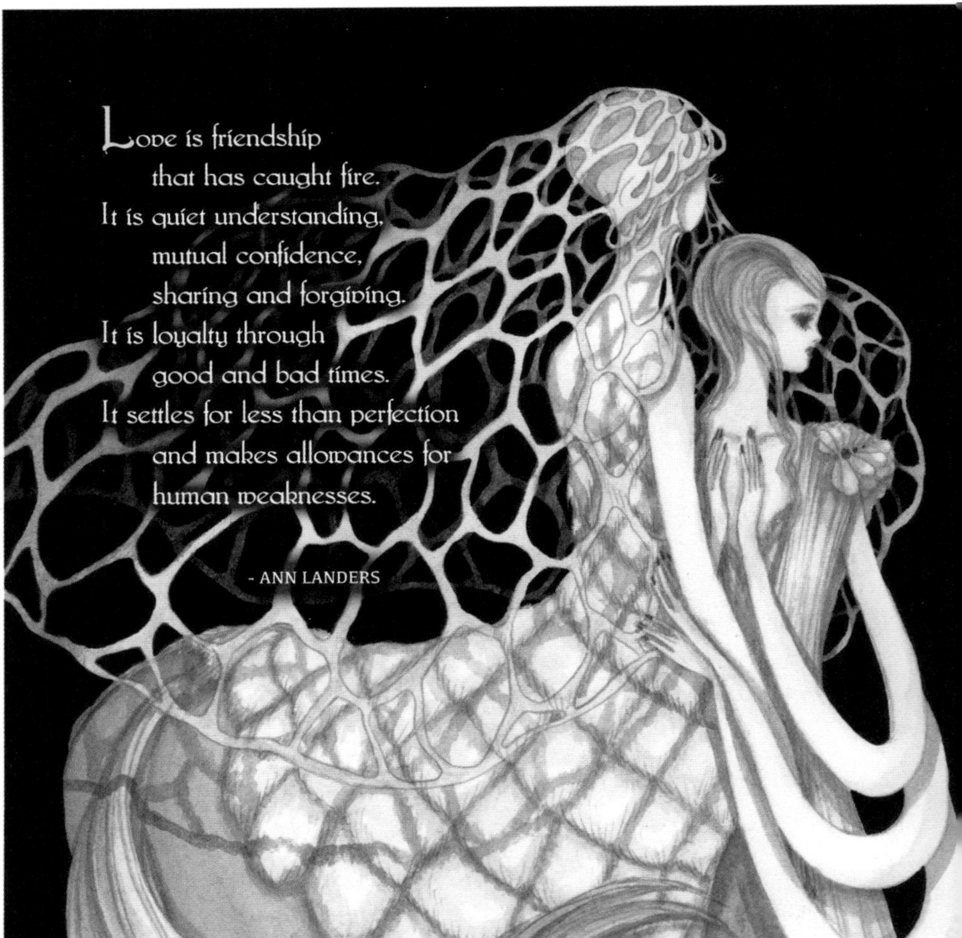
Love is friendship
that has caught fire.
It is quiet understanding,
mutual confidence,
sharing and forgiving.
It is loyalty through
good and bad times.
It settles for less than perfection
and makes allowances for
human weaknesses.
- ANN LANDERS

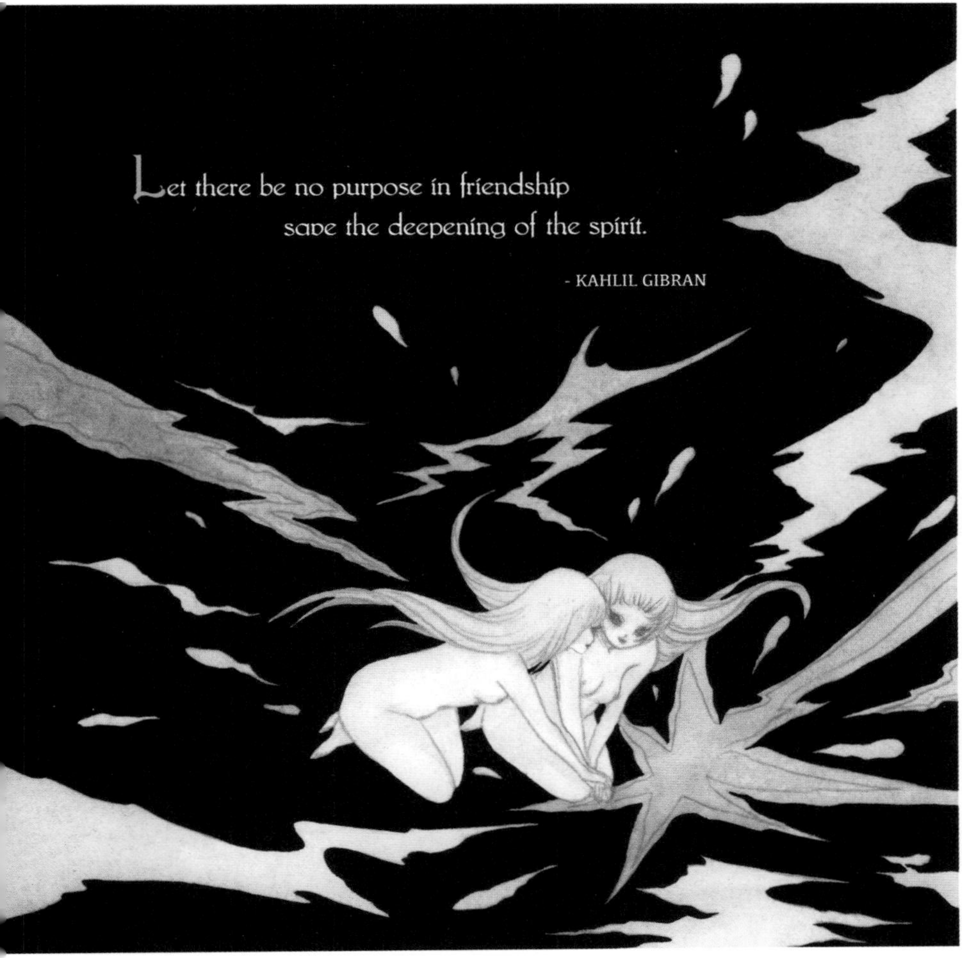
Let there be no purpose in friendship
save the deepening of the spirit.
- KAHLIL GIBRAN

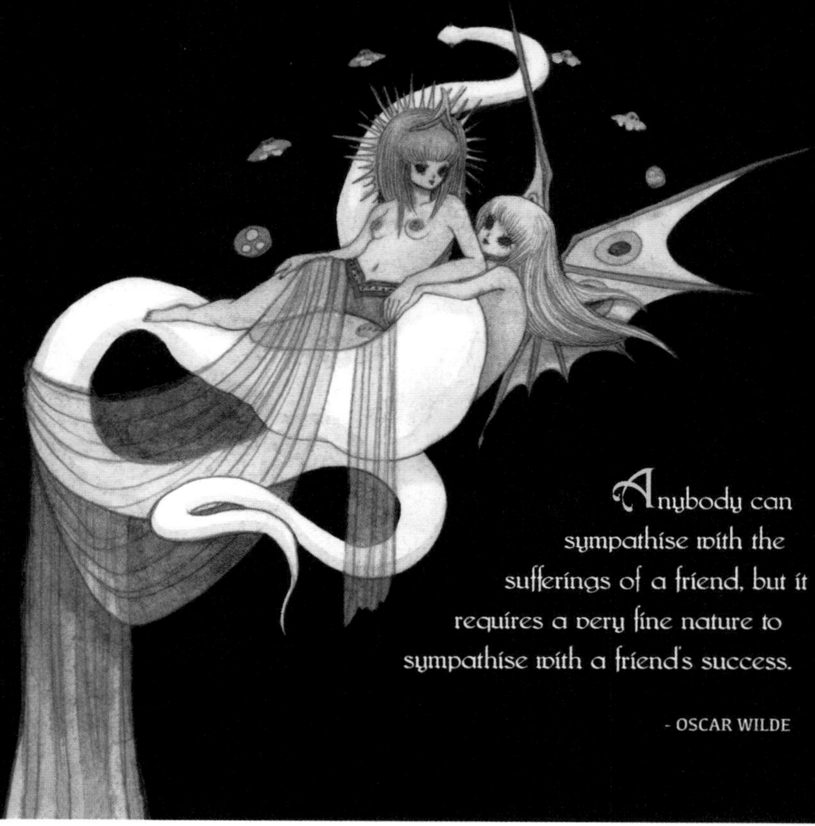

Anybody can sympathise with the sufferings of a friend, but it requires a very fine nature to sympathise with a friend's success.

\- OSCAR WILDE

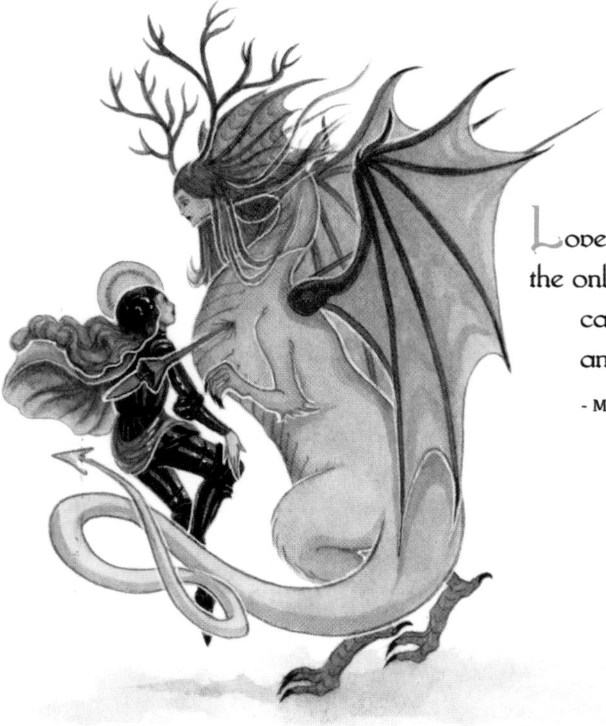

Love is
the only force
capable of transforming
an enemy into a friend.

- MARTIN LUTHER KING, JR.

My friends have made the story of my life. In a thousand ways they have turned my limitations into beautiful privileges.

- HELEN KELLER

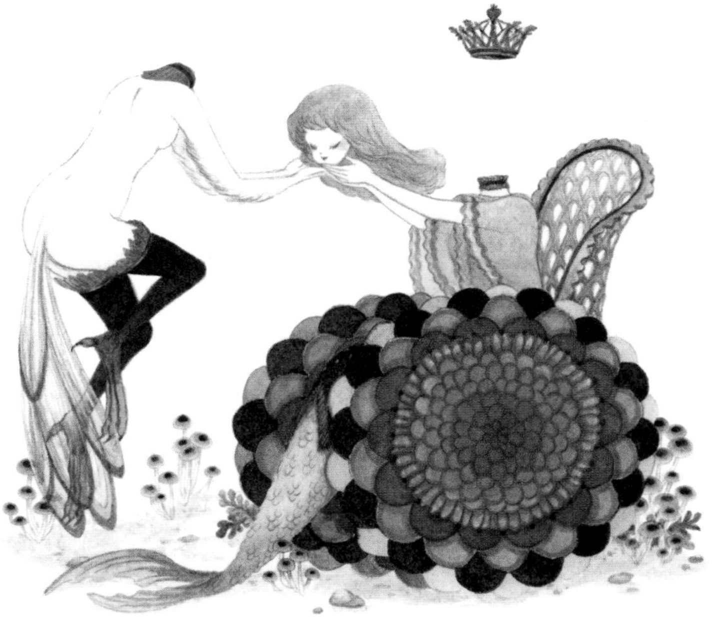

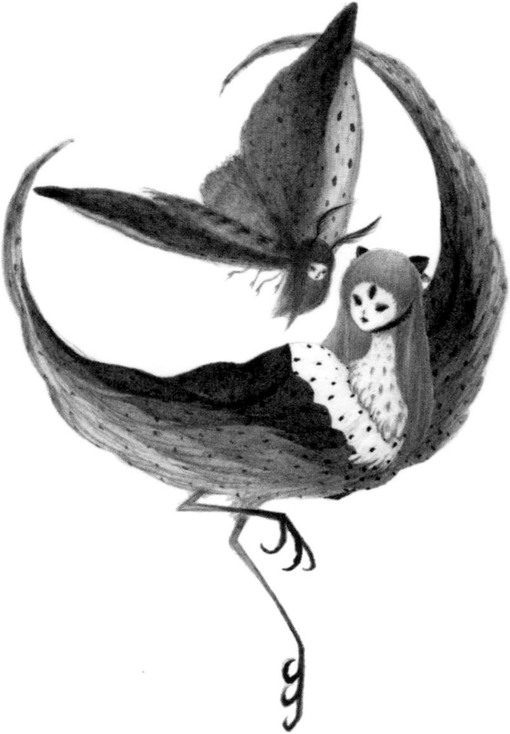

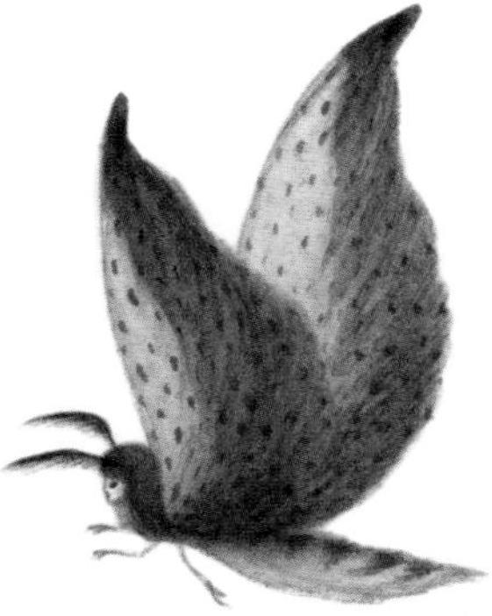

What is a friend? A single soul dwelling in two bodies.

- ARISTOTLE

My definition
of a friend
is somebody who
adores you
even though they
know the things
you're most
ashamed of.

- JODIE FOSTER

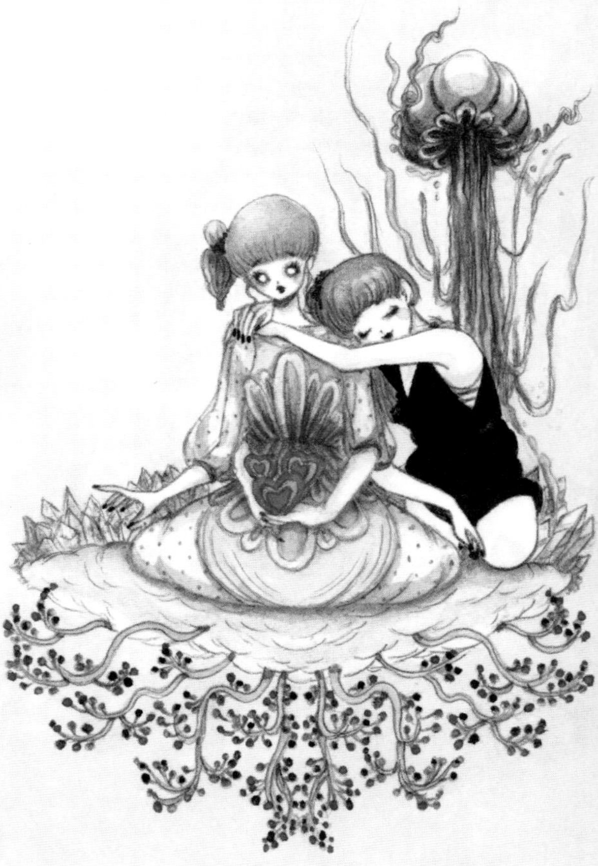

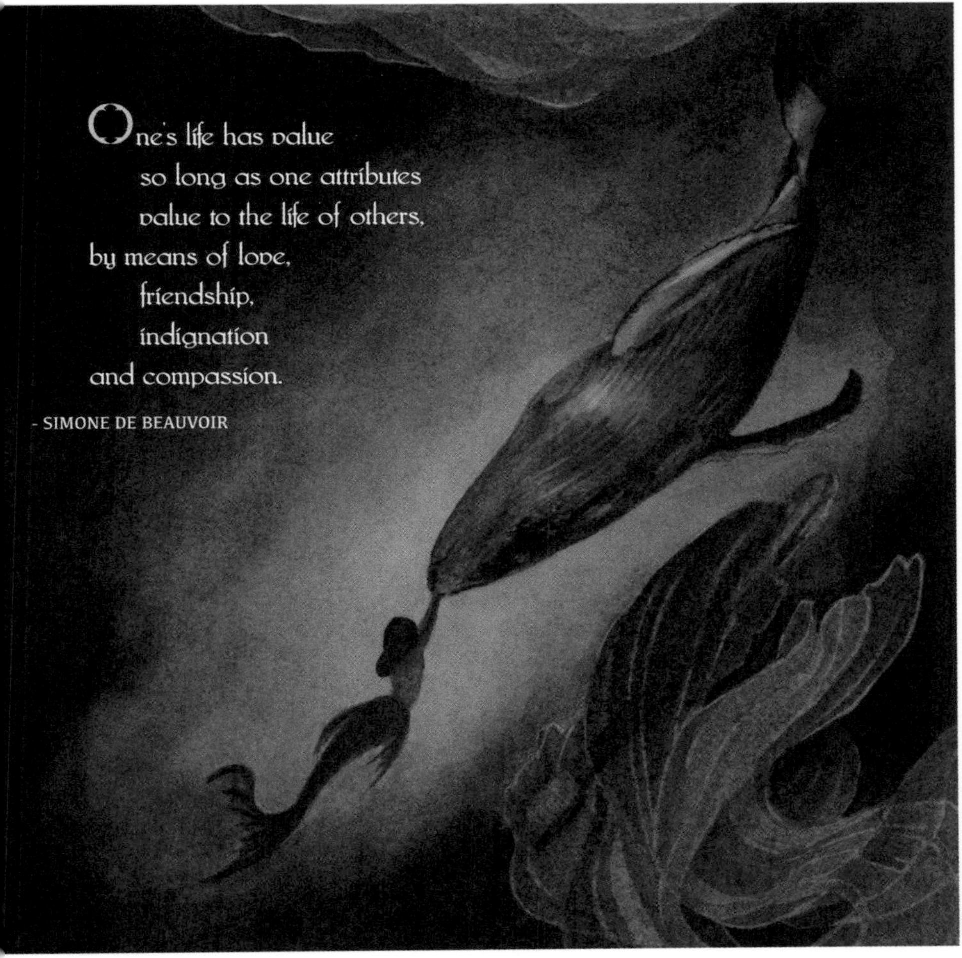

One's life has value
so long as one attributes
value to the life of others,
by means of love,
friendship,
indignation
and compassion.

- SIMONE DE BEAUVOIR

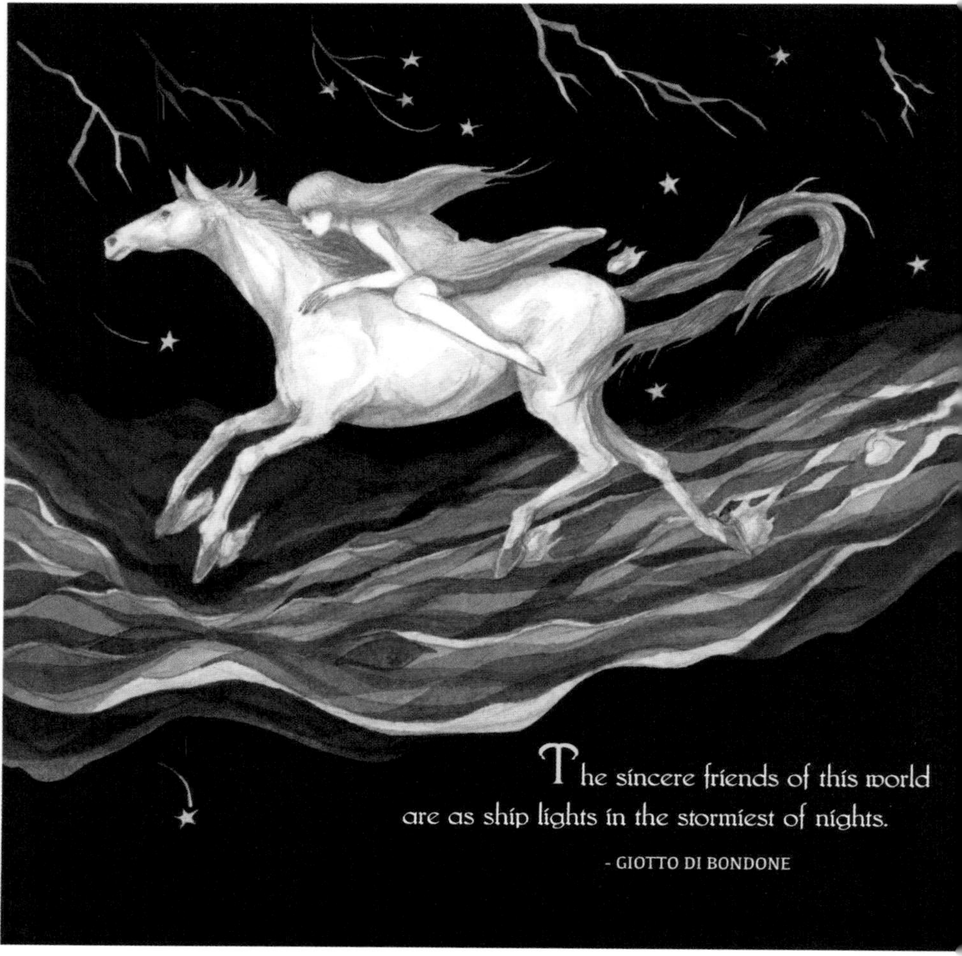

The sincere friends of this world
are as ship lights in the stormiest of nights.

- GIOTTO DI BONDONE

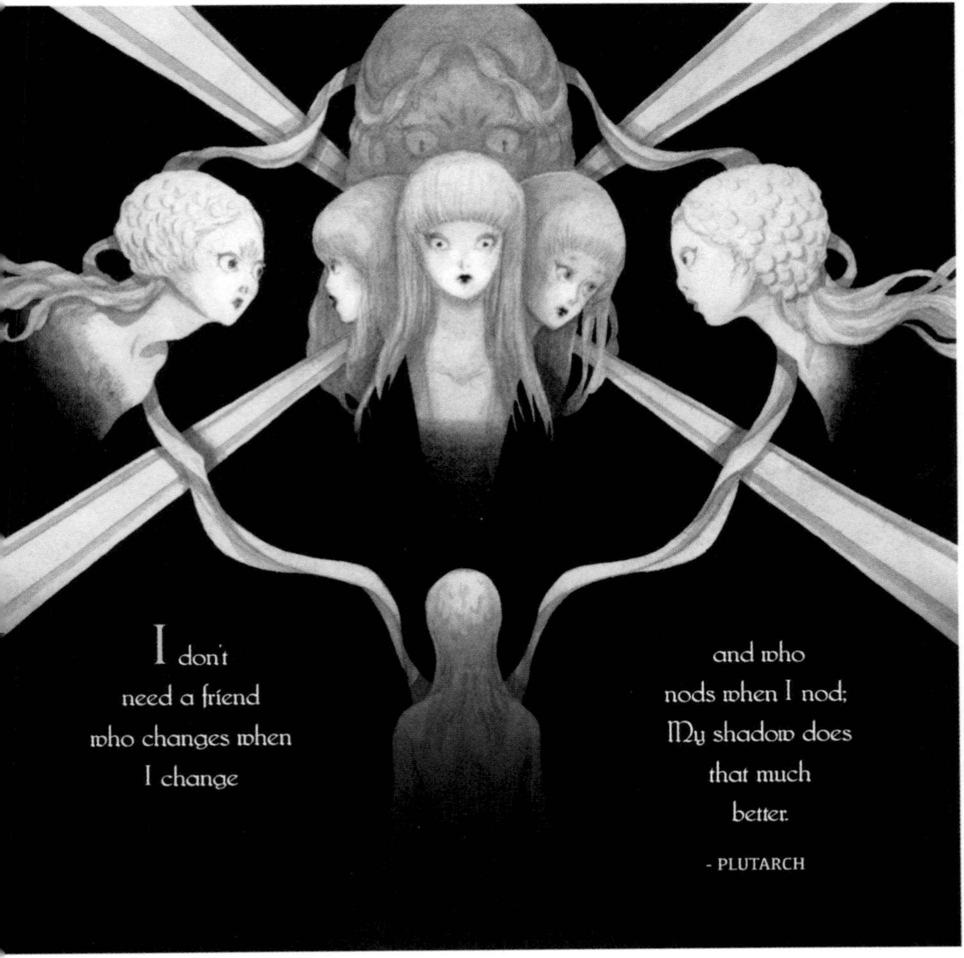

I don't
need a friend
who changes when
I change
and who
nods when I nod;
My shadow does
that much
better.

- PLUTARCH

T is the privilege
of friendship
to talk nonsense,
and to have have
her nonsense
respected.

- CHARLES LAMB

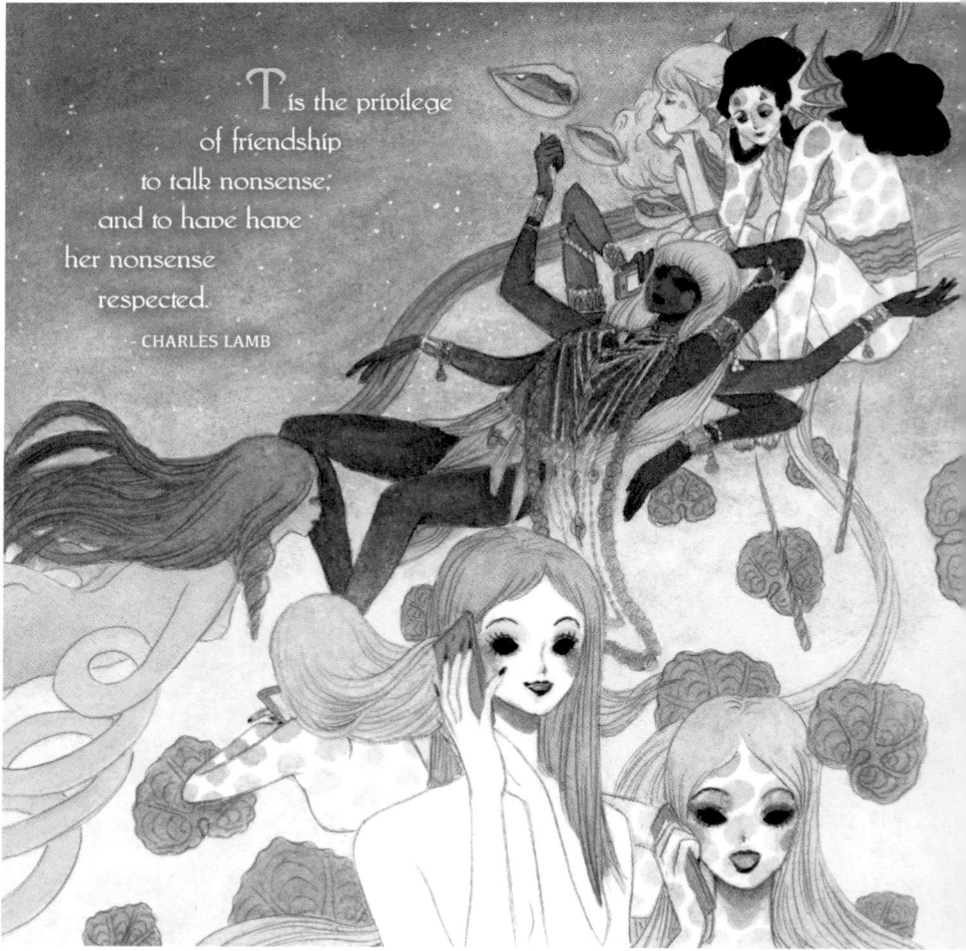

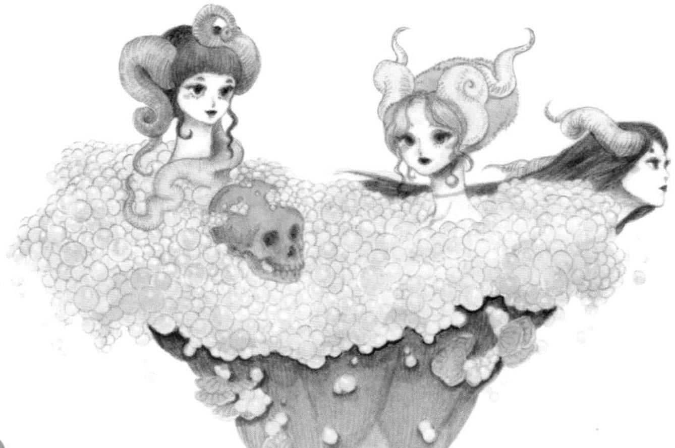

Only hang around people that are positive and make you feel good. Anybody who doesn't make you feel good, kick them to the curb.

And the earlier you start in your life the better.

The minute anybody makes you feel weird and non-included or not supported, you know, either beat it or tell them to beat it.

- AMY POEHLER

No good friends, no bad friends;
only people you want, need to be with.
People who build their houses in your heart.

- STEPHEN KING

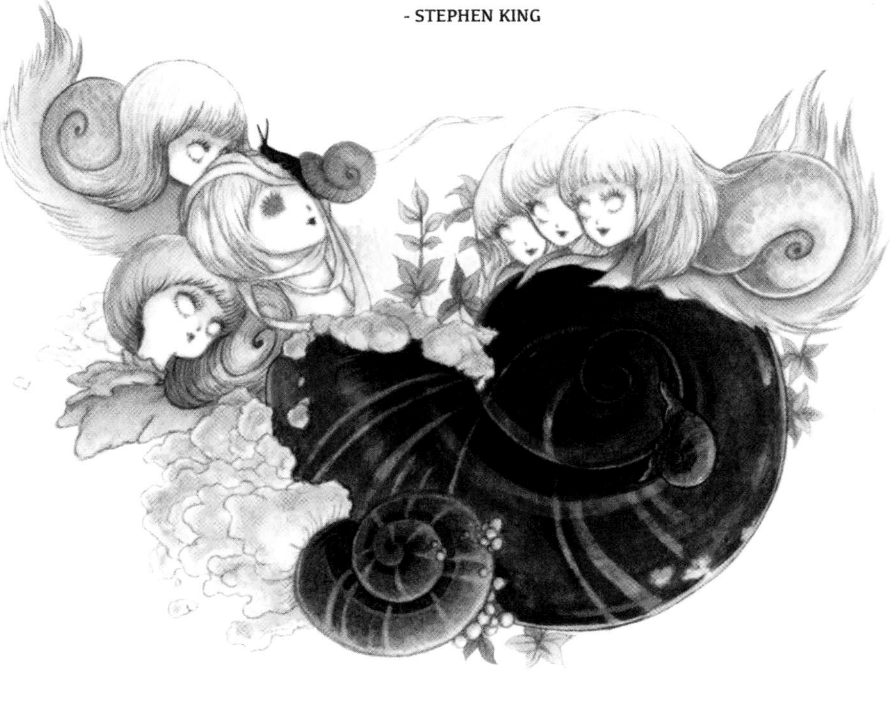

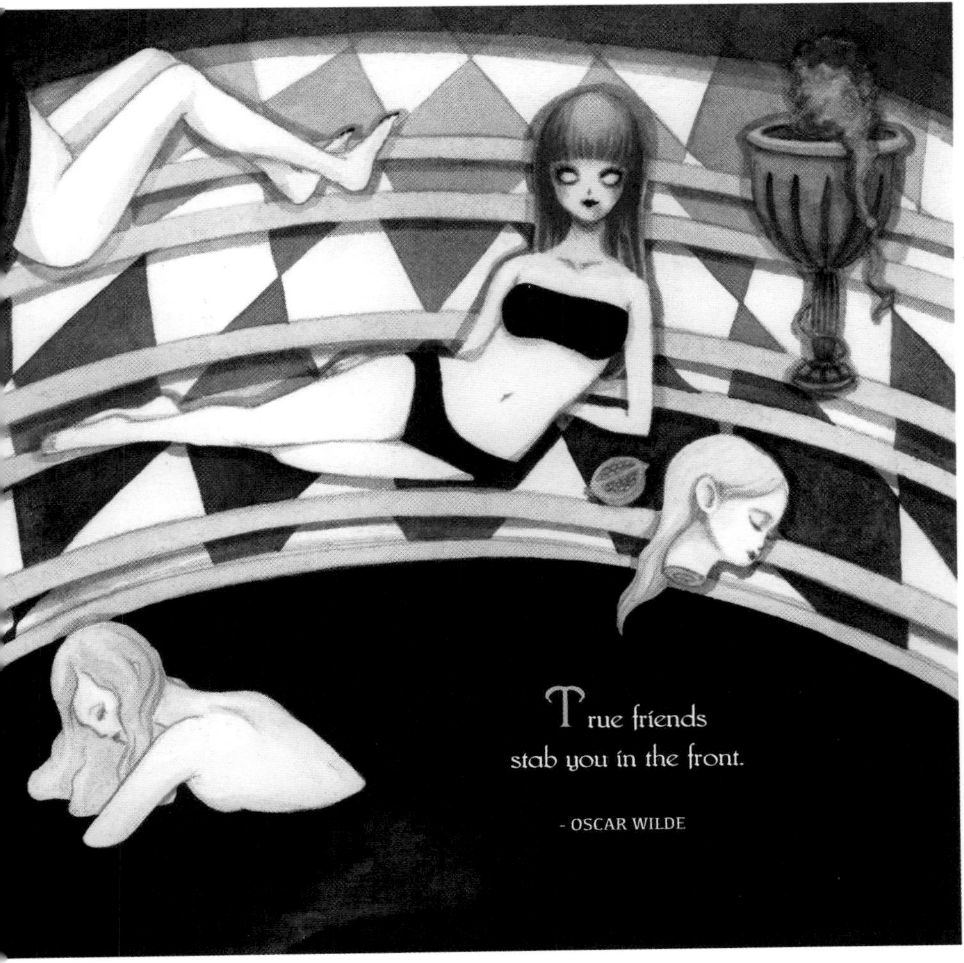
True friends
stab you in the front.
- OSCAR WILDE

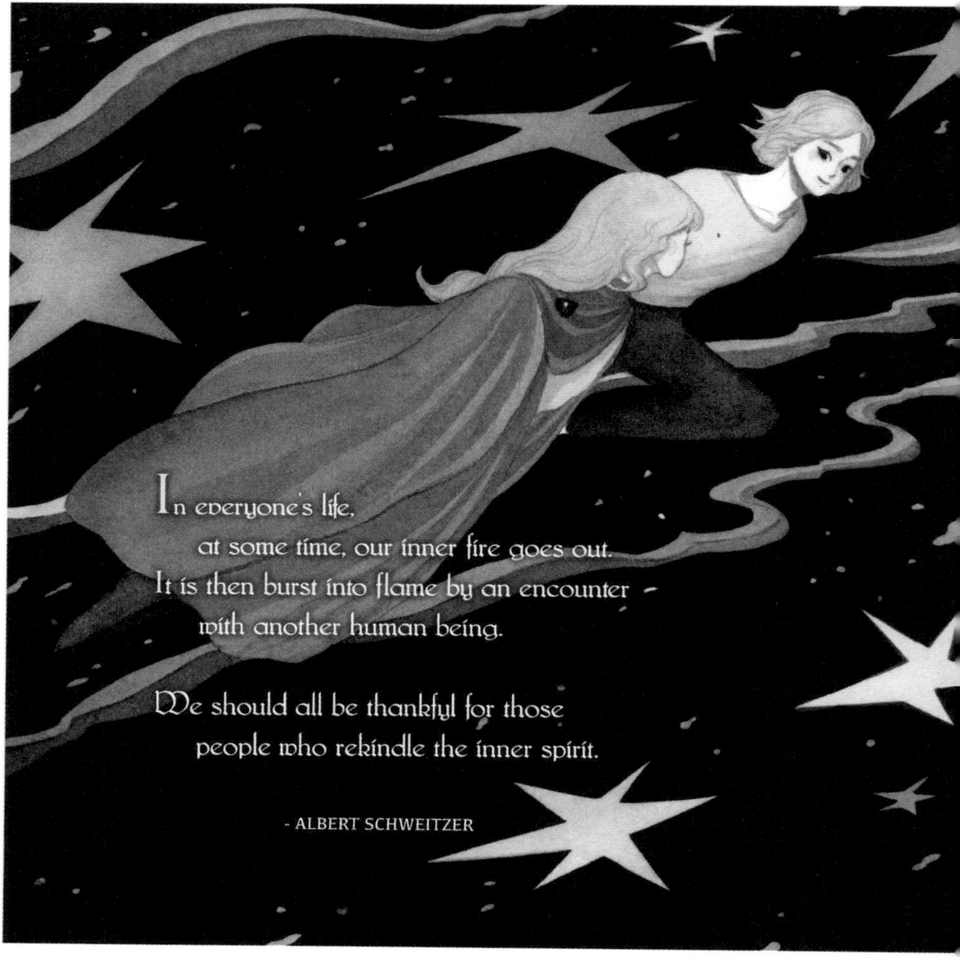

In everyone's life,
at some time, our inner fire goes out.
It is then burst into flame by an encounter
with another human being.

We should all be thankful for those
people who rekindle the inner spirit.

- ALBERT SCHWEITZER

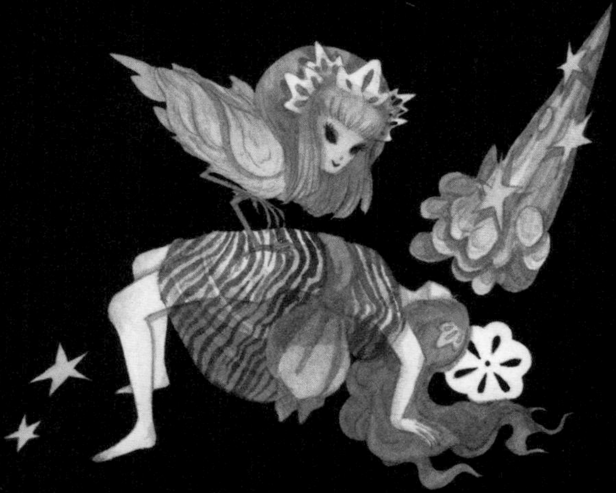

Friendship with oneself is all-important, because without it one cannot be friends with anyone else in the world.

- ELEANOR ROOSEVELT

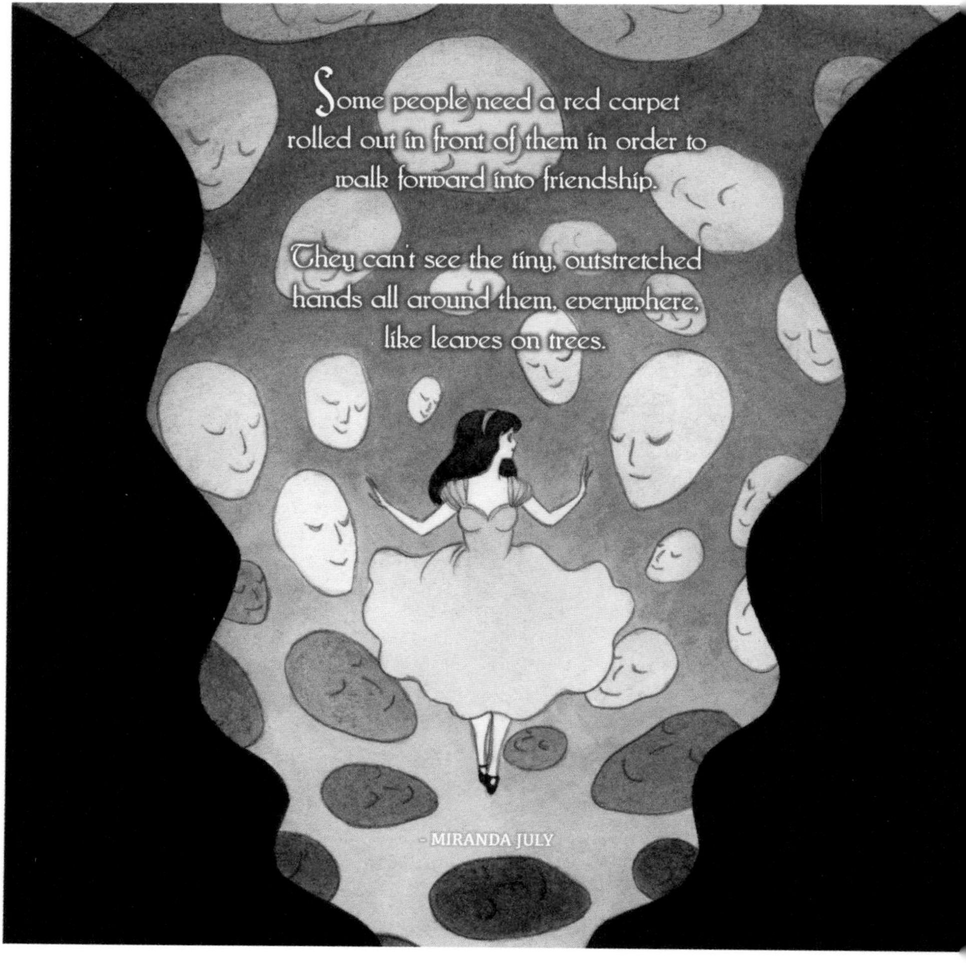
Some people need a red carpet rolled out in front of them in order to walk forward into friendship.
They can't see the tiny, outstretched hands all around them, everywhere, like leaves on trees.
- MIRANDA JULY

No distance of place or lapse of time
can lessen the friendship of those who are
thoroughly persuaded of each other's worth.

- ROBERT SOUTHEY

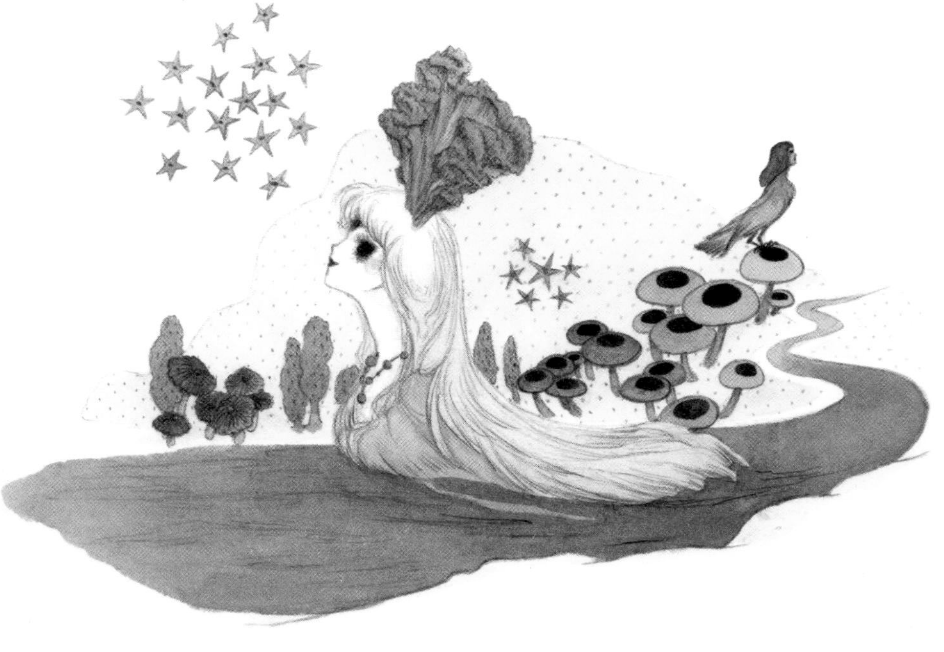

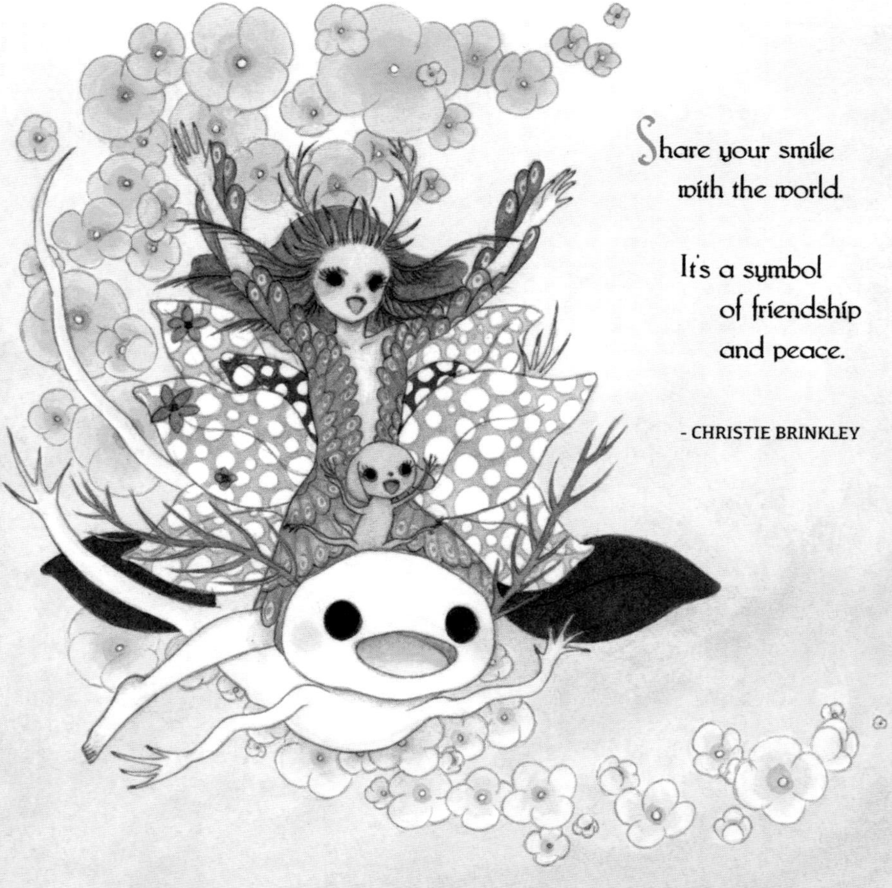

Share your smile
with the world.

It's a symbol
of friendship
and peace.

- CHRISTIE BRINKLEY

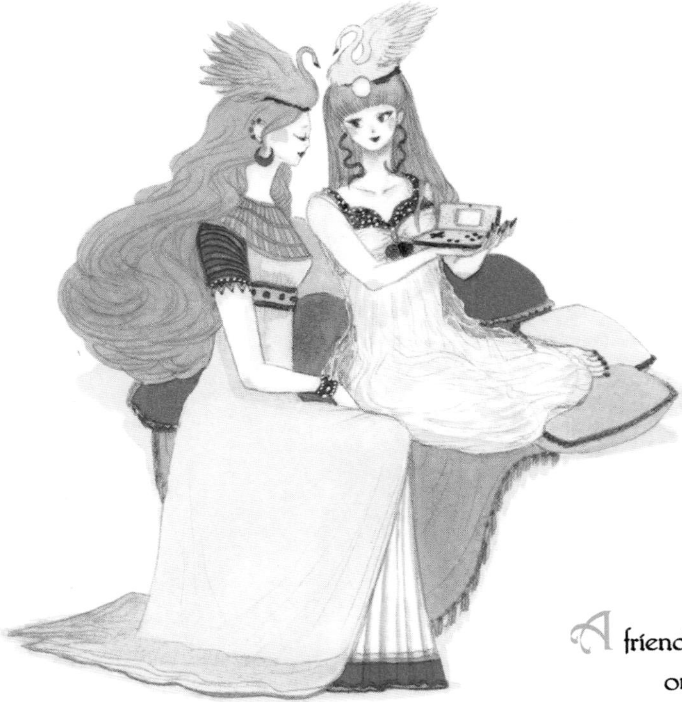

A friend is
our alter ego.

- ZENO

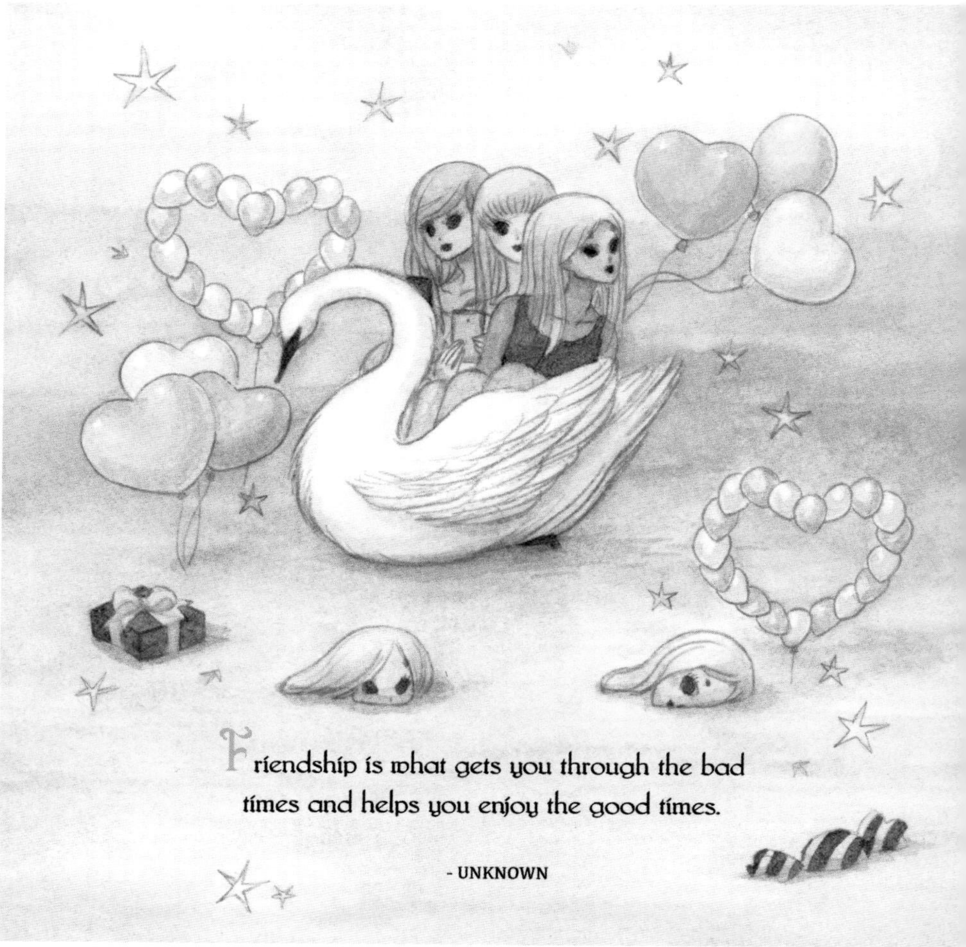

Friendship is what gets you through the bad times and helps you enjoy the good times.

- UNKNOWN

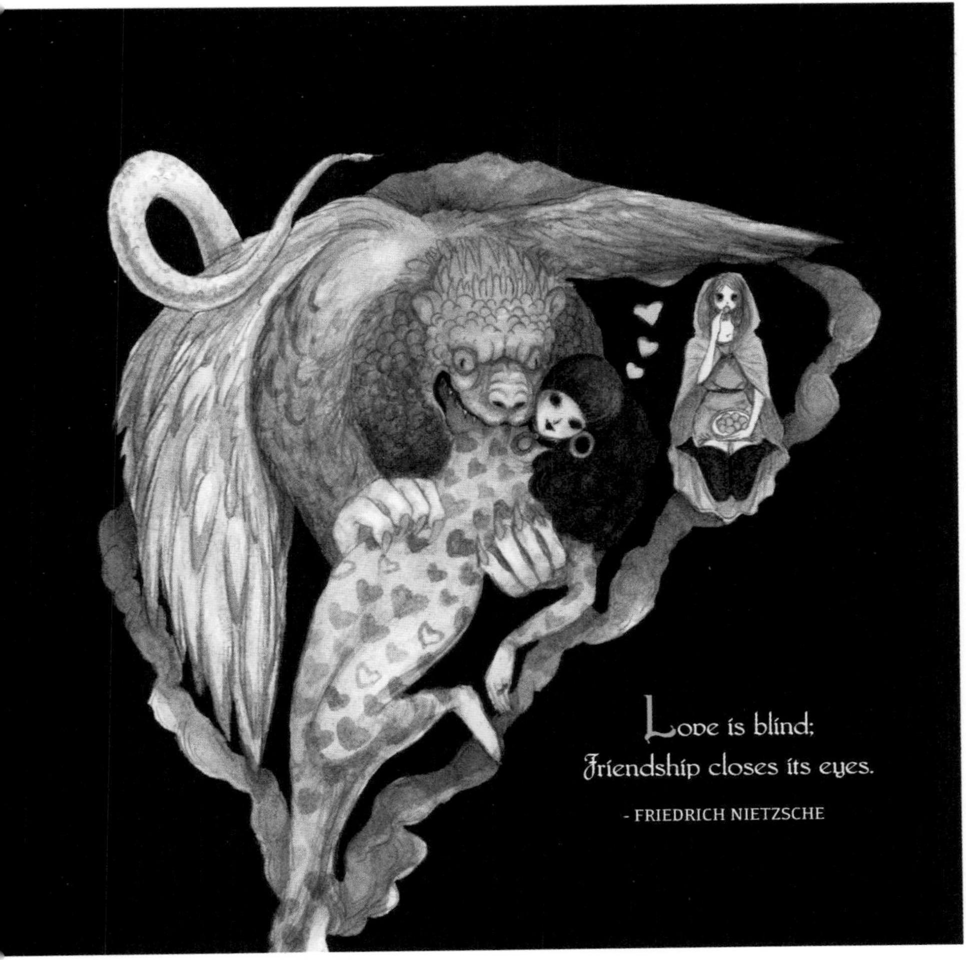
Love is blind;
Friendship closes its eyes.
- FRIEDRICH NIETZSCHE

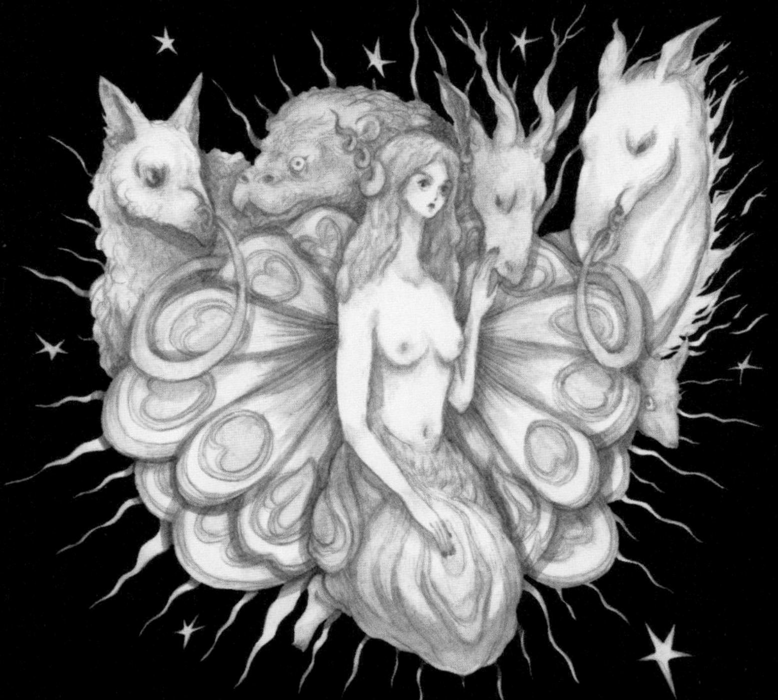

I have perceiv'd that to be
with those I like is enough.

- WALT WHITMAN

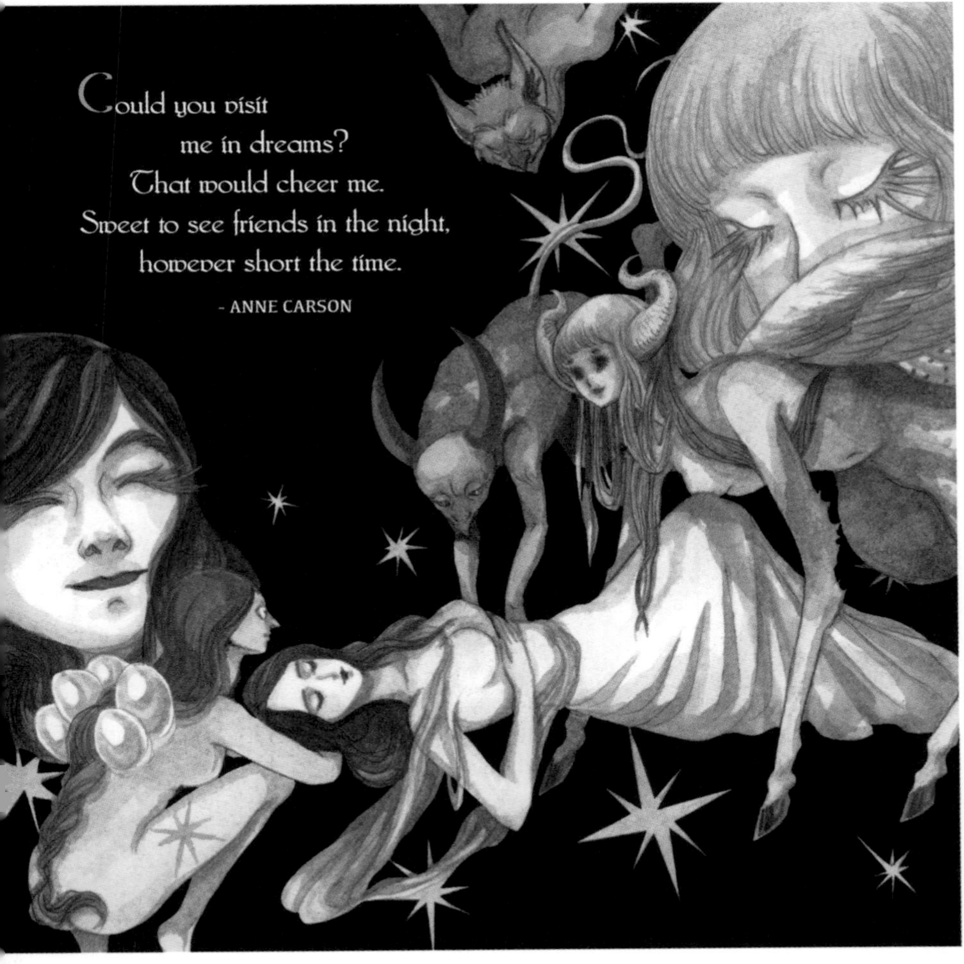
Could you visit
me in dreams?
That would cheer me.
Sweet to see friends in the night,
however short the time.
- ANNE CARSON

I see everyone happy in here,
and I think, "Why
can't that be you"?

- DANI DYER

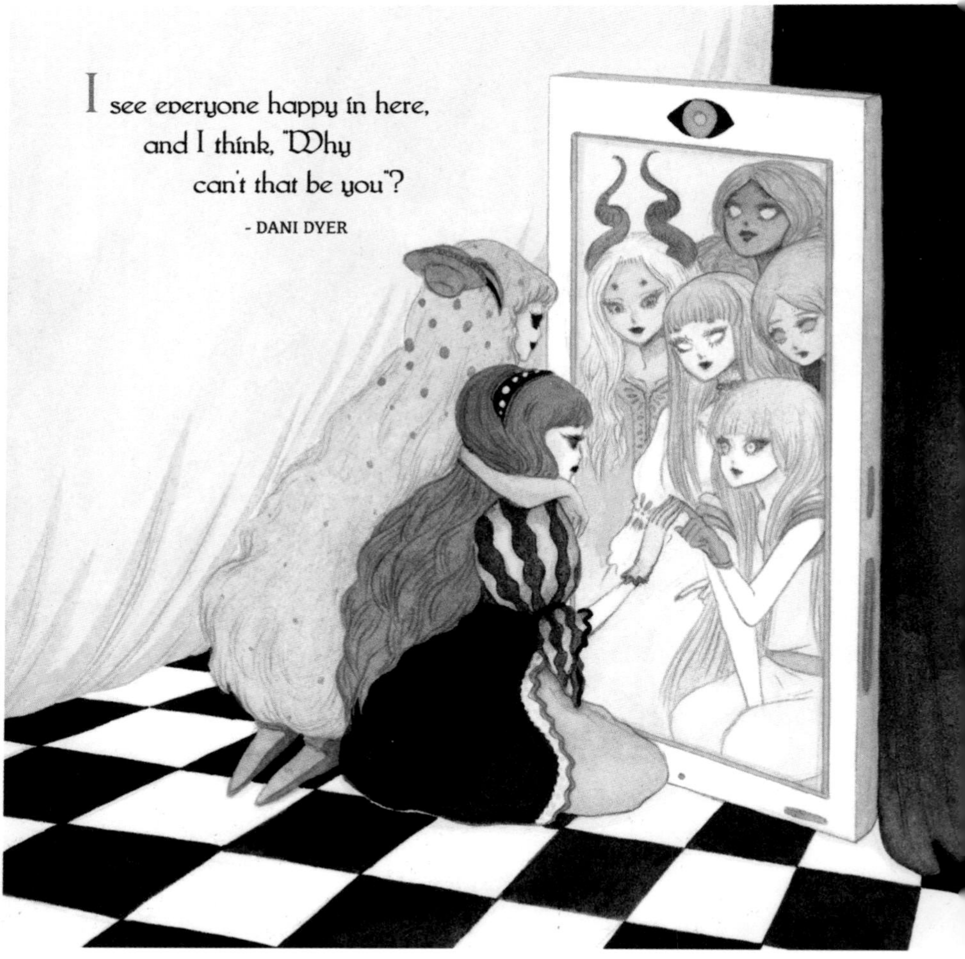

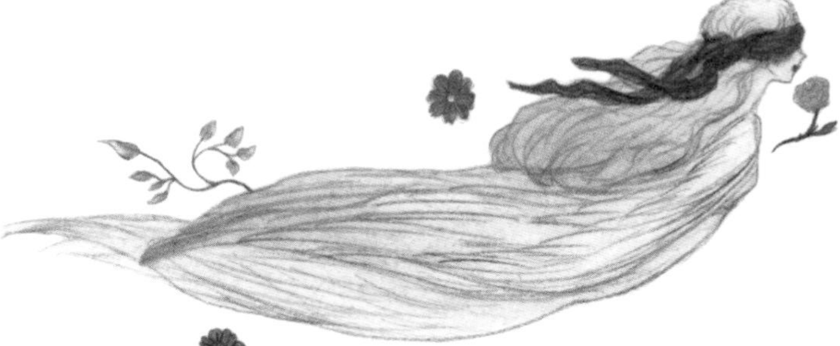

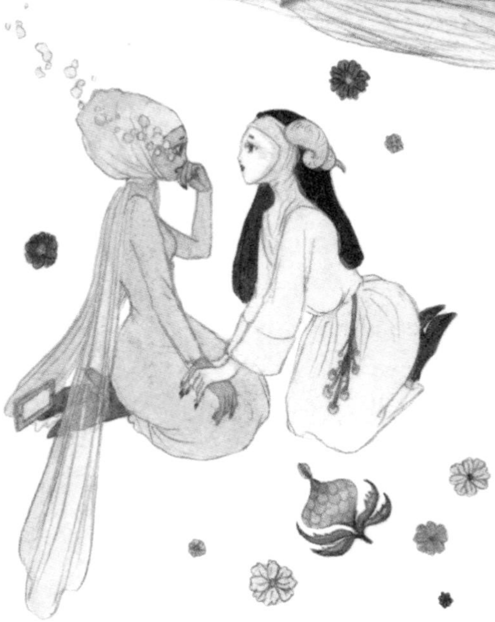

The friend who
holds your hand
and says the
wrong thing

is made of dearer
stuff than the one
who stays away.

- BARBARA KINGSOLVER

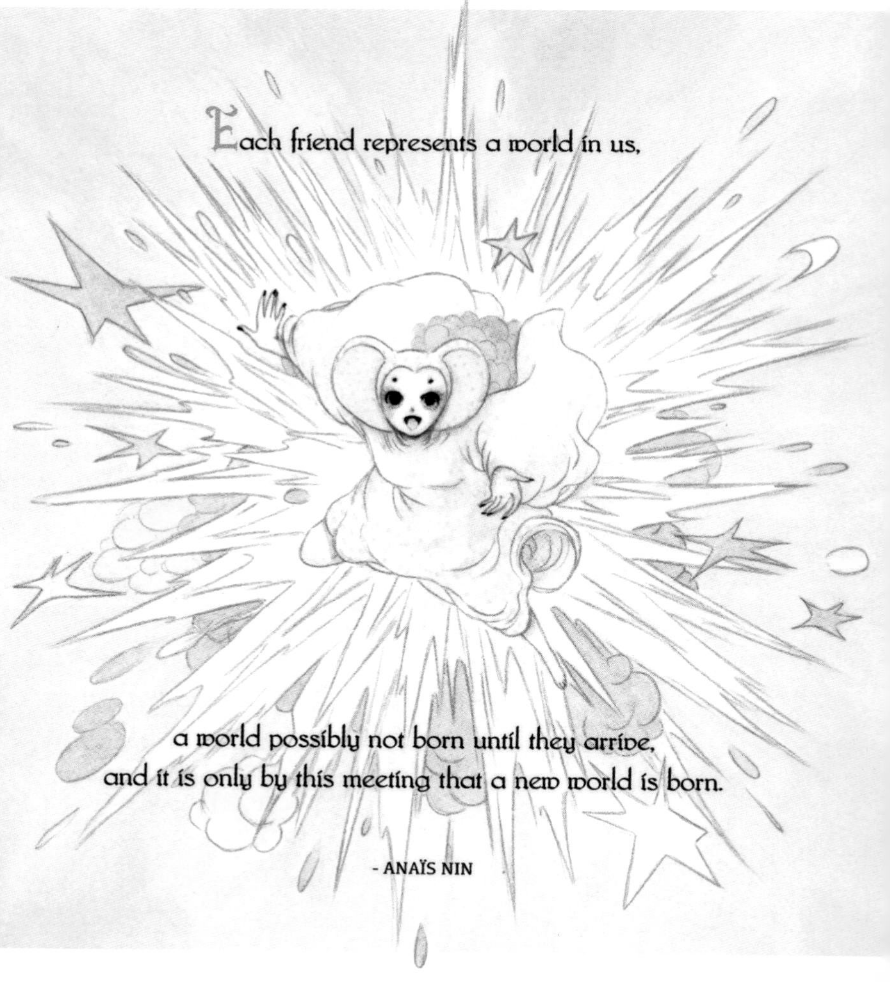

Each friend represents a world in us,

a world possibly not born until they arrive,
and it is only by this meeting that a new world is born.

- ANAÏS NIN

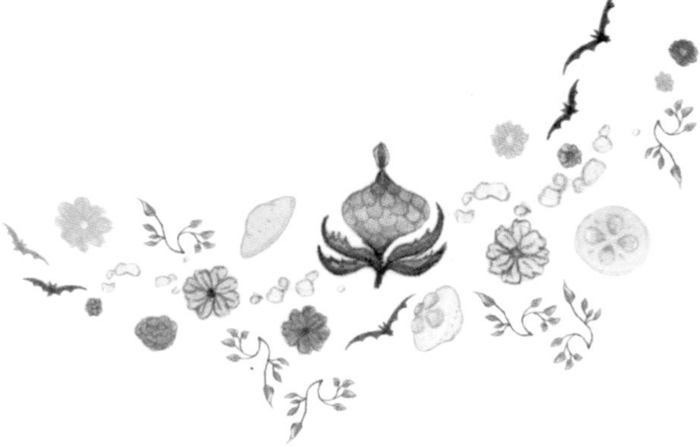

Also in the Mini Meditations series:

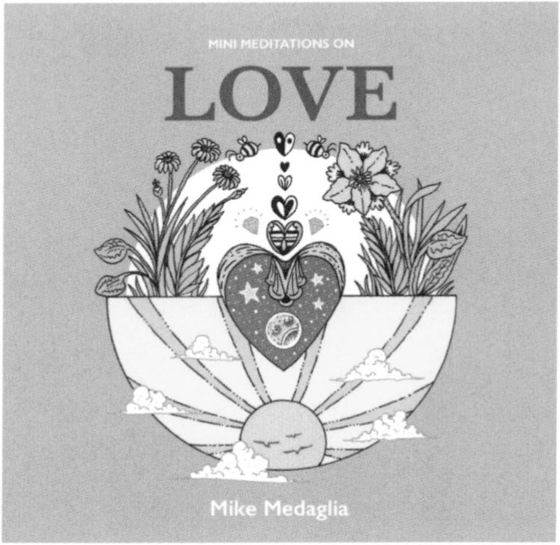

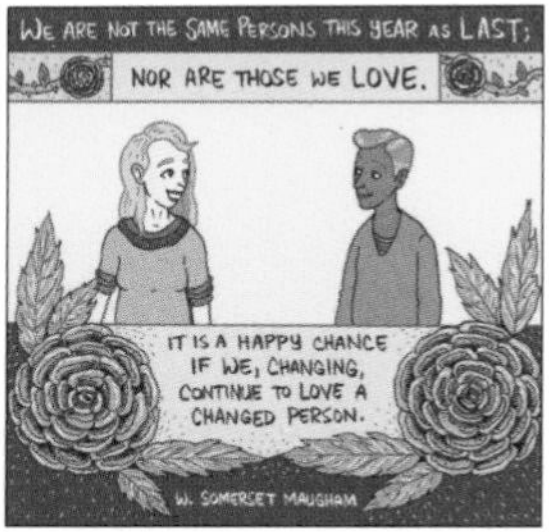

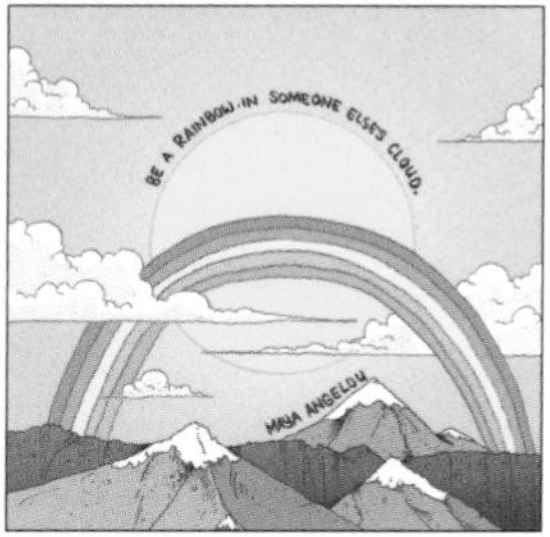

In *Mini Meditations on Love*, Mike Medaglia delves into the thing that drives us all – Love. From the profound to the soppy, every inspirational quote is brought vividly to life through beautiful full colour illustrations!

ISBN: 978-1-912634-08-8

light at the crossroads